The Township of Chorlton-cum-Hardy

The Horse and Jockey when the Green, with a hedge round was still Miss Wilton's garden.

The
Township
of
Chorlton-cum-Hardy

By

JOHN M. LLOYD
(An Old Chorltonian)

1972
E. J. MORTEN (Publisher)
Didsbury, Manchester
England

Published 1972
E. J. MORTEN (Publishers)
10 Warburton Street, Didsbury
Manchester, England

ISBN 0 901598 26 7

Printed in Great Britain by
Scolar Press Limited, Menston, Yorkshire

CONTENTS

FOREWORD

The Rev. John Booker and Thomas L. Ellwood have long been the sole historians of Chorlton-cum-Hardy. The former's 'History of the Ancient Chapels of Didsbury and Chorlton' was published in 1857 when the township had scarcely started to react to the explosion in area and population of neighbouring Manchester which, as much as anything, was the result of improving communications*, and the latter published his 'History of Chorlton-cum-Hardy' in serial form in the South Manchester Gazette during 1885–86.

In the thirty years between the publication of these two works, the march of progress (if such it can be called) had made its mark. Already many of the old cottages for which Chorlton had been well known had been demolished and new houses had been erected in their place, but there was still much of the old left and still people whose memories could bridge the gap of time and remember what it had been like in the past.

After Mr. Ellwood's writings were published in the 'Gazette', he produced several shorter versions for insertion in church bazaar handbooks but all showed unmistakable evidence of their common origin. Since the turn of the century no works of any depth have been published, and it is to complete the story to the present day, as well as to correct some of the errors of the past which otherwise might become accepted as fact, that this work has been undertaken. It is appreciated that in any story such as the one to be unfolded here, there must be gaps in our knowledge and that theorising must sometimes be resorted to; in such cases the reader is entitled to draw, from the evidence submitted, his own conclusions if they differ from those of the author.

It is intended that this shall be a 'Popular' History in the sense that the Victorians used the expression to denote a work designed to appeal to the widest possible audience. To this end

---

* The network of suburban railway services were developing rapidly at this time. The Manchester South Junction and Altrincham Railway through Stretford was opened on 20th July 1849 and omnibus services, many ultimately to become part of the John Greenwood group and through him the Manchester Carriage and Tramway Company, were springing up.

it has sometimes been necessary to venture outside our strict geographical boundary in order to present a coherent story.

The Manchester Local History Library has proved a rich hunting ground, particularly of the late XIX and the present century. Much help and valuable encouragement has been given by the members of the Local History class at Barlow Hall Evening Centre and specialist help has come from Arthur Kirby, the Rev. D. Bonser, and Canon Sewell amongst others.

The 'Old Chorltonians' who congregate each night in the vault at the Trevor Arms have provoked many new lines of enquiry and discovered old pictures and new facts.

I have, without shame, used the excellent researches of Mr. Ivor R. Million, LL.B., for his 'History of Didsbury' (1969), and am equally indebted to the late Mr. W. K. Fox, whose records of Old Stretford have much to offer the historian of Chorlton.

Too often it is said that one history book is very much like all the rest. The limits imposed by the nature of the work, by space, by convenience to the user and by the expense of printing and publishing very often make this true. It is sincerely hoped that the arrangement of the present work will prove acceptable to those who think of themselves as 'Old' or 'New' Chorltonians.

In making the selection of photographs, some restriction has been imposed by the suitability of the originals for reproduction. The picture of the Horse & Jockey when the Green was still Miss Wilton's garden with a hedge round it demonstrates the condition that comes of being kept, for nostalgic reasons, for many years in handbags or wallets.

Most of the pictures have been loaned for copying, some of which have been copies themselves, and consequently it has not always been possible to make proper acknowledgement. When, through ignorance, no acknowledgement appears, it is sincerely hoped that this apology will be accepted.

The author will always appreciate the opportunity of copying photographs of the township, and he can be contacted most conveniently through the publishers.

ABBREVIATIONS

The term 'township' is used to refer to the loosely defined area which was to become Chorlton-cum-Hardy in later years.

. . . .

Abbreviations used in the genealogical tables:

dau.	Daughter.
d.	Died.
b.	Born.
ch.	Baptised.
int.	Buried.
m.	Married.
s.	Son.
sis.	Sister.
inf.	Infant.
w.	Widow.

. . . .

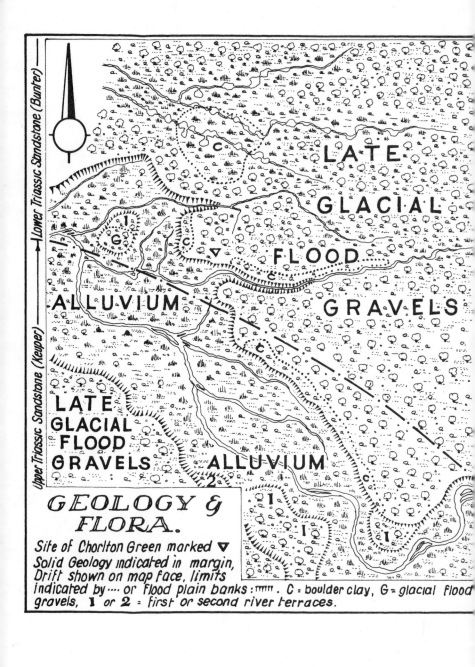

GEOLOGY &
FLORA.

Site of Chorlton Green marked ▽
Solid Geology indicated in margin,
Drift shown on map face, limits
indicated by···· or flood plain banks: ⋏⋏⋏⋏. C = boulder clay, G = glacial flood
gravels, 1 or 2 = first or second river terraces.

Chapter One

IN THE BEGINNING

Ellwood states, uncompromisingly, that Chorlton was founded in the year A.D. 610. This date is without any authentic support[1] and, in fact, the foundation of the township might have been at any time between then and A.D. 900.

What is known in this 'dark age' is that the Anglo-Saxons, who had settled along the eastern seaboard of Britain soon after the departure of the Roman occupiers, and some were already here around 410 when the evacuation took place, slowly extended their occupation and by the end of the sixth century were penetrating the Pennines. These movements, and to some extent their associations, can be traced by the names by which the settlements became known; it being a reasonable assumption that the first infiltration through the Lune Valley in (*c.*) 570 originated near Tyneside, for there is an apparent link between names like Melling and Pilling in Lancashire and Felling near Newcastle.[2]

Similarly the second movement in (*c.*) 600, largely through the Wharfe/Ribble valleys gave us the 'ing(a)ham' form—compare Whittingham near Preston with Billingham in Co. Durham.[3]

Sometime around 615 came a third movement, this time producing settlements of the 'ing(a)tun' group[4] through the Calder/Roch valleys. It would be nice if these settlements were confined to the valleys through which the movements had occurred but those of the 570 infiltration can be found in the Ribble valley and those of the 600 one in Cheshire. Thus a nice tidy group of ing(a)tuns (Partington, Warrington, Dumplington, etc.) have an intruder in the form of Altrincham.[5]

It is to the post-615 movement that we owe the foundation of Chorlton. We do not know when but whereas the two earlier movements had been reasonably peaceful, the third was made as the result of military action. Perhaps the British felt that the time had come to resist the intrusion or, perhaps, King Ethelfrith of Bernicia (Northumbria) was militarily minded. We know that he had by this time conquered Deira (Yorkshire) and his conquest of the west culminated in the battles of Degsaston (603) and Chester (615).

It is unfortunate that the picture of Anglo-Saxon Britain presented through the usual history books seems to be that existing south of a line running roughly from Shrewsbury to Lincoln, for the beginnings of Chorlton cannot be seen in that context. The more southerly regions of Britain had been intensively cultivated under the Romans and were therefore ready to maintain a considerable number of the immigrants from across the North Sea, so much so that many areas could be shared between two communities and two lords. The north of Britain on the other hand, had had little attraction for the Roman farmer; much of the land was quite unsuited to cultivation and the climate was no better then than it is now. This, together with the fact that it had been a military zone throughout the occupation meant that there was little other than rough and wooded land.

The nearest approach of the Romans to the site of the future Chorlton was the road from Deva (Chester) to Mamvcivm (Manchester) which crossed the Mersey at Stretford and, remotely possible, a minor road through Northenden.[6]

The ancient forest of Arden occupied both sides of the Mersey, the principal trees being the oak and the willow. The river itself had a wide bed which it fully occupied in times of flood but which at other times was a damp marshy area through which a shallow sluggish stream meandered. Variations in water level were then much greater than they are now for no water was extracted in the higher reaches to feed mills and reservoirs, nor was there any compensation water in times of drought. Evidence of the old limits of the flood plain is still clear to see though recent tipping of waste suggests that little will remain to be seen in a few years time.

The path from Brookburn road down into the Meadows on the way to 'Jackson's Boat', the sudden dip in Hawthorn Lane as it winds round the backs of the houses built on the old 'town tip', the quick fall behind the houses along Edge Lane and behind Barlow Hall School are all visible signs. In ancient days the river was well-known for the unpredictable speed at which it would flood. When the first attempts to control the course by means of artificial banks were made is not known, but it may well be that the first primitive guides were erected before the

Conquest. It seems unlikely that the earliest settlers were unaware of the rich deposits of mud which were brought down by the floods and that they would not try to exercise some control over them.

The geological picture of the township is simple. The underlying solid rock is Bunter and Keuper sandstone and Keuper waterstone with deposits of late glacial flood gravels and alluvium. North of the river are deposits of boulder clay.

We can assume, with tolerable certainty, that an Anglo-Saxon family[7] settled in the area and proceeded to make clearings (tun) wherein to grow their crops and live out their simple lives. The family centre of this group was Withington (wittinga-tun = the enclosure of the family of WIDEA (or WITEGE), or the tun amongst the (osier) willows. With ample land available the group fragmented and established their dominion over a large area, probably including what was later to become Didsbury, Burnage, Rusholme, Levenshulme, Denton, Haughton, and part of Moss Side as well as Chorlton. This was the area covered by the later Manor of Withington, a sub-manor of the post-Conquest Manor of Manchester, but probably older than its superior.

The order or the date at which the various communities were established is unknown but the Anglo-Saxon origins of the four elements of the ancient township of Chorlton are quite clear.

To consider them in detail we start with Chorlton. This is based on either CEORLA-TUN = the enclosure of the ceorls or peasants or, according to the Concise Oxford Dictionary of Place Names, on CEOLFRIP-TUN = Ceolfrip's enclosure. A ceorl was the lowest rank of freeman, a level below the thane and above that of the serf. The centre of Chorlton was where the village green stands and it will be seen later that in the Middle-Ages it still showed some of the character of its Anglo-Saxon form.

Hardy occupies the south side of the Chorlton Brook (or Gore Brook as it is known in its higher reaches) and derives its name from Ard (=a wood or a tree, c.f. Arden)[8] and ea (= water or a river). This latter element is found associated with water in several forms. It appears on old maps and plans to indicate land liable to flood and as such Sale Ees still appears on the current 1 in. Ordnance Survey map 101. (ref. 798928). Whilst Chorlton Ees has now disappeared it was shown on early maps (e.g. 1 in. O.S. of 1843) as that area later occupied by the Withington U.D.C. Sewage Works. Sometimes the word has been modified to 'Eye' and as such can be found in Park Eye (which was where Princess Parkway now crosses the Mersey), or, alternatively, as Park Eea.

Martledge was the third part of the township. Its derivation is more obscure and the number of different ways in which it has been rendered through the ages has not made it any simpler to understand. It would seem most likely to originate from its position on the northernmost boundary of the township (or of the domain of Withington), Mæres = boundary, and the wet nature of the ground, lache = pool(s), marsh or lake. This part of the district is on a deposit of boulder clay which restricts drainage. Old maps show a succession of pools along the course of the Black Brook and the Longford Brook from Barlow Moor Road/Manchester Road (which in the XIX century was known as Martledge) through to Longford Park. This area, now occupied by Longford, Newport and Nicholas Roads, was known as 'The Isles' and within living memory there was a considerable brickworks bordering Longford Road. Martledge as a community can be defined as the locality of the Barlow Moor Road–Manchester Road Junction, and as an area, from the railway to Longford Park and Wilbraham Road to West Point.[9]

Before the Protestation of 1641 a fourth part of Chorlton Township was Hughend (now Hough End), and though later a part of Withington, it is so much concerned with events in Chorlton, and is so generally accepted as part of 'Chorlton-cum-Hardy' that it is felt sensible to so consider it. It lay to the east of the present St. Werburgh's Road, south of Chorlton Brook to Barlow Moor Road and then to the east of that road. This is a rough delineation, a more accurate definition will be given later.

Again the derivation of the name is not clear enough for there to be unanimity of opinion. Until recently it had been generally accepted as a description of a dwelling (= hof, possibly that of the lord) near the boundary of Withington and Chorlton (= ende). It is more likely that the boundary would be that of the settlement in its broader sense but the likely explanation is that 'ende' refers to a part or area of the manor so that a literal translation would be 'the part in which the house of the lord is situated'.

The township, for though we are not sure when it was granted this status (Elwood states 'ten years later. . . .' (than 610!), it is convenient to so refer to the area, was on the Northumbrian side of the boundary river (Mæres - ea). The Sale side was Mercia but about 923 Edward the Elder, son of Alfred the Great, pushed the Mercian boundary northwards to the Ribble. He divided the new territory into six 'hundreds' and so positioned Chorlton and Manchester in the Royal Hundred of Salford.

A mystery surrounds the Nico, Great or Mickle Ditch. This is usually considered to extend from near the boating lake in Platt Fields (853945) to Debdale Park (901960) and so does not come within the bounds of this work, but the 6 in. Ordnance Survey map, sheet SJ89SW, marks a short length of the course of the Longford Brook between the railway (north of Stretford Station) and Rathbone's Boat Yard (801948) as part of the Ditch. This would mean that the in-between length would strike through Martledge. When this ditch was constructed, for it is clearly man-made, is not known. Tradition has it that it was dug by the Anglo-Saxons in a single night and certainly it is probably of their doing for they were great diggers of ditches to mark boundaries. It might be later but it is mentioned in an Audenshaw deed of 1200 and certainly it marks a fairly accurate northern limit of that part of the Manor extending from Platt to Debdale. If it was a manorial boundary it passes out of the Manor in going into Stretford and there is the other curious feature that somewhere it would have to pass obliquely across the Gore Brook. It is not mentioned by Crofton in his History of Stretford Chapel nor in Booker's History of the Chapels of Didsbury and Chorlton (though, strangely, Booker does not mention it in his History of Birch Chapel either) and, all in all, it is probable that there is no justification for thinking that it had any connection with the township or that it extended to any extent westward from Platt Fields.

So we end this first phase of our story with the four constituents of Chorlton-cum-Hardy tilling their own separate enclosures and probably quite unaware of events of far reaching importance that were happening elsewhere.

6 THE TOWNSHIP OF CHORLTON-CUM-HARDY

NOTES

1 Possibly because Whittaker refers to A.D. 610 as the date when '. . . the neighbourhood south of Manchester was disencumbered of its ancient oaks.'

2 Probably 'fælging' Œ newly cultivated land, 'Mellingas' Œ the people of Moll or Malla.

3 'Ingaham' Œ the homestead of. . . .

4 'ingatun' Œ the enclosure (home) of. . . .

5 The home of 'Aldhere's people' or 'the home on the top of the hill.' which is a fair description of the site of old Altrincham.

6 This is based on the discovery of an alleged Roman road in the 1930s when some alterations were being made to some shop property. A reference to a Roman road which would be a continuation of the same line occurs in 'A History of Withington' by Kenneth Whittaker, pps. 7-8 where he claims evidence of such a road along Birch Lane, Rusholme, to Birch Hall and then to Burton Road/Barlow Moor Road corner.

7 This would be more of a tribe than our modern concept of a family.

8 Whittaker notes that the area south of Manchester retained the name of Arden, or 'great wood' for ages.

9 The wall across the end of Grange Road marks the later defined boundary.

The original Chapel, 1512-1779, from Booker's History of Didsbury and Chorlton Chapels.

St. Clement's Old (Parish) Church, churchyard and Lych Gate.
The old Bowling Green Hotel in the background. (source unknown).

St. Clement's Old (Parish) Church, west end, from Hawthorn
Road (now Ivygreen Rd.) (comm. p.c. ref. L 5013).

TO THE MEMORY OF
NICHOLAS COCK

Headstone from the grave of P.C. Cock as it now stands at County Police H.Q. at Hutton, Preston. (photo. author).

The Old Bowling Green Hotel, demolished 1909. (original in the Hotel, courtesy the landlord).

The Horse and Jockey Inn before the imitation 'black and white' was applied. Photo. c. 1900. (source unknown).

The Green, Chorlton-cum-Hardy.

The Green about 1904 with the horse 'bus for the Prince of Wales waiting to depart. A fountain stands where there is now a 'phone box. (comm. p.c., probably Saxony).

Brook Farm where now is the Express Dairy depot. Prob. c. 1905. (comm. p.c. ref. 5022).

Chapter Two

A NEW AGE

Chorlton township passed into a new age. The Domesday Inquest which recorded that 'King William holds all the lands between the Ribble and the Mersey which Roger of Poitou held. . .' found no need to chronicle the township or its value and probably the villagers were quite unaware that they had been the subject of what we would today call a 'take-over'.

Whatever its previous status, Withington eventually became a sub-manor of Manchester. In the Great Inquest of June 1212, which records lands in Lancashire and their holders:

'Mahthew son of William, and Roger, son of William, hold the fee of one knight of Robert Gredle in Withington of ancient time, and must find a judge for the King.'

suggests that as the Manor was 'of ancient time' it was possibly older in establishment than Manchester and therefore pre-Conquest. This is emphasized by the requirement to supply a judge for the King since, in pre-Conquest times, Salford (being a Royal Hundred and Manchester as a Manor not being then established) the King would be the direct overlord of Withington. It is obvious from the extract that by 1212 the Lord of Manchester Robert Gredle (i.e. Grelle) had imposed his suzerainty and was exacting his fee.

Somewhat later in that same century Withington was still in the possession of William de Withington but later it was granted by Robert Grelle to Matthew de Hathersage in return for one knight's fee. Ivor Million in 'A History of Didsbury' contends that William de Withington had sons Matthew (the Mahthew, son of William, quoted) and Roger. This Matthew was the Matthew of Hathersage, which is perfectly feasible as surnames as we know them did not exist and 'de Hathersage' or 'de Withington' did not indicate family but only where they lived.[10]

By the end of the XIII century the Manor had passed to the Longford family though by what precise means is not clear. Again relying on the researches of Ivor Million, Matthew de Hathersage passed the Manor on to his son Matthew who had two daughters, one of whom, Cecilia, married Nigel de Long-ford, and the other, whose baptismal name is not recorded, married Gousil de Barlborough who may have also been known as Simon de Gousil.

It may be that there was a period when Simon de Gousil and/ or John Byrom were lords of the Manor. The Lancashire Assize Rolls quote Simon in both 1276 and 1278 but the inquisition post mortem of Robert Grelley, 1282, names John de Byrom as holding the Manor for the term of his life. Sir John Longford, either because he was the grandson of Nigel (who married Cecilia) or because he married Joan the daughter of Sir John de Byrom, whose ward he was, had become Lord by the end of the XIII century.

In the survey of 1300 the knight's fee had been exchanged for a monetary payment:

'Nicholas de Longforde, for one fee in Wythington, homage fealty and suit of court, worth 6s 8d, paying for sake 9s and for ward 10s and putary serjeant and arms or armour.'

This payment continued unchanged throughout the occupancy of the Longfords until 1593 when financial difficulties forced Sir Nicholas Longford to sell, for £2,100, to Sir Robert Cecil, Hugh Beeston, Michael Hicks and Humphrey Flint:[11]

'The Jurye dothe presente that Nicholas Langforde esquier hath soulde to the Ho: Sir Roberte Cycell knighte to Mr Hygh Byston esquier et als, the Lordshippe of Withington, and that ye sayde Sr Roberte Cicell & the sayde Hughe Byston et alls are to come and doe theire sute and service.' (Manchester Court Leet records, session of 2nd October 1595).

The payment probably continued to be paid but the Manor again changed hands on 13th December 1597 when Roland Mosley purchased it and brought it under the same family control as the Manchester Manor. At this point the payment probably ceased.

Chorlton as a situation is mentioned in 1148 when, in the twelfth year of the reign of King Stephen, Gospatric de Chorlton granted lands in that part of Chorlton called Beswick[12] to the Abbey of Cokersand (sic). This is probably the same Gospatric who is mentioned in the statements on the de Trafford family (Harleian MSS. already noted in footnote 10) where:

'Henery his sonne (of Rafe de Trafford) by this Stile rec^d from Heleas de Pendlebercie in Gildhusteeds (Rusholme), for (i.e. from) Gospatricius de Chorleton in Chorleton, fro D. Ham' de Mascy in Stretford, . . .'

This extract is taken from H. T. Crofton's 'History of the Ancient Chapel of Stretford' (Vol. III, p. 99 *et seq.*) and he quotes a parallel record from John Corry's History of Lancashire (1825):

'Robertus, filius Radulphi, fillii Radulphi de Trafford.[13] Hee lived in William Rufus his tyme and the beginning of Henry first his raigne about the year 1120. He left a sonne called Henry (who) by this stile received lands from Helias de Pendlebury in Guildersted, from Gospatrick de Chorlton, from Hamo(nd) de Massey in Stretford, from Adam de Cheetham neere the river Medlock, from Matthew Fitz Guilielmi. . . .'

Again from Crofton:

'This Henry de Trafford, by that only name, received lands from divers; viz: from Thomas de Hyde in Sale, from Nigel de Longford in Withington, from the Abbot of Cocker-sand in Chorlton and Bexwicke, anno Dom. 1200, from Richard Fitz None in Stretford, from Roger de Pendlebury in Yieldhouses, from Matthew Fitz Gulielmi in Aldehulme, from Robert de Chorlton in Chorlton, and many others . . . . Hee lived in the end of King Steeven his raigne, and in the raigne of Henry the 2nd and Richard the 1st untill about the year 1190 or thereabouts as appeareth by deeds to him granted. He left a son called Rich. He died Ad. 1200. . . .'

From another of the Harleian MSS. (2112 fol. 137) Henry de Trafford's five bovates of land in the township were held on payment of six shillings and three pence.

Gospatric (de Cherletona) appears in another (undated) deed of about the same time with a grant to. . . .

'. . . Henry, son of Robert, son of Ralph de Trafford, of one fourth part of Chorlton, namely four bovates of land with appurtenances; to wit two bovates which Ralph held, one bovate which Steinulph held, and one bovate which Robert, son of Edwin held, with all woods, plains, pastures, clearings, mills, &c., and all liberties and easements to that township belonging: to hold the same to himself and his heirs from him, the said Gospatric and his heirs on payment of five shillings per annum, namely, fifteen pence at the Nativity, fifteen pence at Easter, fifteen pence at the feast of John the Baptist, and fifteen pence at the feast of St. Michael.' [14]

The deed is witnessed by Roger de Burun, Orm de Astun, Robert de Burun, Matthew de Redish, William de Radcliffe, Roger de Middleton, Adam de Buri, Gilbert de Notona, William his son, Geoffrey de Burun, Hugh de Stretford, Alexander de Pilkinton, Matthew de Glothet, Hugh de Soresworth, and Robert his brother, Robert, son of Hugh de Mascy and others.[15] The names and styles of the witnesses to these deeds are interesting in themselves; while it is clear that security of tenure was enhanced by numbers one is left to wonder how such a gathering could be arranged in those days of poor communications.

Probably as a result of the transference of land to the Abbey of Cockersand some hundred or so years earlier (though some, if not all would seem to have been conveyed to Henry de Trafford, as just noted) we find the Abbot of Cockersand claiming privileges in Chorlton and Wythington of waifs, infangenthef and the assize of bread and ale. Respectively the claiming of things found astray, the judging of a thief arrested within the lord's fee (land) and the checking for weight and quality. These rights, together with exemption claimed for himself and his monks from fines and amercements appertaining to the Crown were disputed by the officers of the Crown and the Abbot, being unable to submit evidence strong enough to persuade the inquisitors, had his claim rejected.

The family of de Chorlton appears again during the reign of Edward I in a deed which is undated but probably pre-1290 when another Gospatric de Choreton seems to have had a dispute with the Lord of the Manor of Withington over land and by the deed gave one eighth part of Chorlton to his brother Adam ' . . . who is about to fight for me against William son of Wulfrith de Withington to secure my right to my estate in Chorlton.' Robert de Burom, Henry de Chetham, Ralph de Moston, Jordan de Norreys and Henry de Trafford are amongst the witnesses. It seems that Adam was unsuccessful in his championship of his brother's cause.

At this time, in the reign of Edward I, Gospatric de Chere-leton held two carucates of land in Cherelton as tenant in chief of the King in thanage and by the payment of twenty shillings. Thanage, the liability for military service, dated from Saxon times and establishes the Chorlton family as being of substance though of rank inferior to the nobility. In Norman times the rank corresponded to that of a knight. A carucate was the amount of land which could be kept under cultivation by one plough in the year and, as a land measure, varied according to the type of land. At this same time Henry de Chetham by the same service and the payment of 5s held from the King four bovates of land; Matthew, son of William tenanted four bovates of the King by knights' service which he claimed by having performed that service on behalf of the King; William de Bothelton held one bovate from the King and Adam de Chorlton held two bovates on payment of 'xlj den.' (41d.)

In 1322, in the fifteenth year of the reign of Edward II, the Survey of the Manor of Manchester records Thomas de Chorl-ton as having seven acres of heath land in Green Lowe Marsh in Gorton by a certain assize of novel disseisin,[16] and a cottage in Ardwick for which he paid no rent, having undertaken to lease it. In this same Survey, Ivor Million, in his History of Didsbury, refers to a Dame Matilda de Chole being concerned with William le Smyth of Diddisburie and Robert de Chedle in the 'disseisure' of one rood of land of the Lord (of the Manor of Manchester).

The boundaries of the Manor of Manchester were to an extent defined as being '. . . between Stretford and Chollerton (which is a member of Withington) as far as Molsfrellach (Martledge); and following that as far as into Withenton clou and Trafford as far as the bounds of Chorlton and Trafford into le Cornbrook.'

The de Traffords were at this time exerting an increasingly strong influence in Chorlton. In the rent-roll of Edmund, Earl of Lancaster, 1316 (Edward II)[17] Henry de Trafford was one of the Earl's tenants in the township, paying an annual rent of 5s Richard Pilkington paid a rent of 20s and Richard de Byrom 24s.

Chorlton at this early period was called upon to make con-tributions to the Lord of the Manor other than their rents and were required to contribute to the maintenance of '. . . the lord's bailiff or sergeant and that of a boy, a horse and four under-bailiffs, supplying to the chief sergeant, when he shall come there, bread, ale, victuals and other things necessary, according to the season, and for his boy and the four under-bailiffs such food as they are accustomed to provide in the house, and provender for his horse, on notice of their coming.'[18]

In 1331–32, in the reign of Edward III, the lay subsidy for Salford Hundred produced £39 4s. Robert de Trafford's contribution for his property in Carleton was 3s 4d and he was the only person assessed in the township. The relative importance of Chorlton and Stretford is indicated by the latter's assessment of 22s. Ten years later, 1341, a commission which met at Preston granted to certain individuals the right to levy a ninth of corn, wool and lambs in every parish according '. . . to the value upon which churches were taxed if the value of the ninth amounted to as much as the tax, and to levy more where the true value of the ninth should be found to exceed the tax'. The necessary information was to be obtained from the residents of the parish on oath and it was at pains to point out that it originated:

'. . . in regard to the will which the king their liege lord hath towards his subjects, and to the great travails that he hath made and sustained as well in his wars of Scotland as against the parts of France and other places, and to the good-will which he hath to travail to keep his realm and maintain his wars and to purchase his rights. Having regard to this they have granted to him the ninth lamb, the ninth fleece and the ninth sheef; and of cities and boroughs the ninth part of all their goods and chattels.'

In the parish of Manchester the places required to make contributions were Salford-cum-Burghton (i.e. Broughton) lij^s, Chetham x^s, Hulm near Manchester x^s, Stretford xlvj^s viij^s, Redyche lij^s iiij^d and Chorlton x^s. The total tax for Manchester amounted to £14. 13s 4d or 22 marks.[19] (One mark = two thirds of a pound, a large sum in those days, hence the frequency of divisions or multiples of this sum in contemporary accounts). In the time of Henry IV, 1399–1413, a lay subsidy assessed Stretford at 26s 8d and Chorlton at 4s.

The name of de Trafford predominates in these early records.

C.L.C. This ticket is not transferable,
and is issued subject to the
Bye-Laws, Regulations and Conditions
stated in the Committee's Time Tables.

AVAILABLE ON DAY OF ISSUE ONLY

Chorlton
TO
FALLOWFIELD

THIRD CLASS Fallowfield   FARE 3d

0406

Ub 1273

The Barlows of Barlow.
(I)

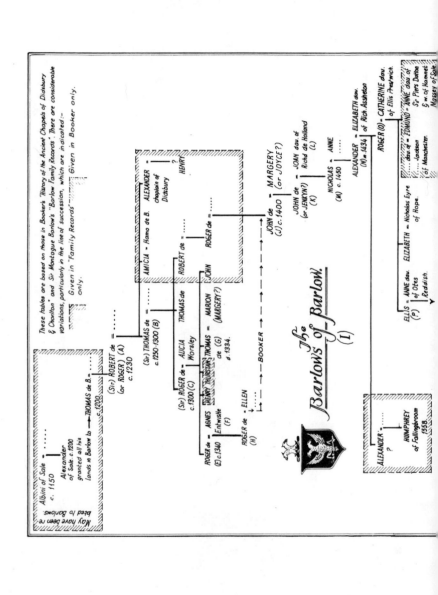

These tables are based on those in Booker's "History of the Ancient Chapels of Didsbury & Chorlton" and Sir Montague Barlow's "Barlow Family Records". There are considerable variations, particularly in the line of succession, which are indicated:—

///////// Given in "Family Records" ///////// Given in Booker only.

Given in "Family Records" only.

Albini of Sale c. 1150 = ...

Alexander of Sale c.1200 granted all his lands in Barlow to ⟶ THOMAS de B. = ... c.1200.

May have been re-bted to Barlows.

(Sir) ROBERT de (or ROGER) (A) c.1230 = ...

(Sir) THOMAS de c.1250-1300 (B) = ...

AMICIA = Hamo de B.   ALEXANDER chaplain of Didsbury

HENRY ?

(Sir) ROGER de c.1300 (C) = ALICIA Worsley

THOMAS de = ...

ROBERT de = ...

ROGER de = ...

HENRY THURSTAN   THOMAS de (G) d 1334.

JOHN

ROGER de = AGNES Entwisle (E) c.1340

MARION (MARGERY ?) = THOMAS

ROGER de = ELLEN (H)

⟶ ⟶ ⟶ BOOKER ⟶ ⟶ ⟶

JOHN de (J) c.1400 = MARGERY (or JOYCE ?)

JOHN de (or JENKYN?) (K) = JOAN dau of Richd de Holland (L)

NICHOLAS = ANNE (M) c.1450 = ...

ALEXANDER (N) m.1434 = ELIZABETH dau. of Rich Assheton

ROGER (0) = CATHERINE dau. of Ellis Prestwich.

ELIZABETH dau d = EDMUND = ANNE dau of Sr Piers Dutton. ...... Jackson of Manchester. & w. of Hamnet Massey of Sale.

ELLIS = ANNE dau of Otes Reddish. (P)

ELIZABETH = Nicholas Eyre of Hope.

ALEXANDER = ...

HUMPHREY of Fallingbroom 1558.

Most tell us little of the township itself but are concerned with litigation. There was, for instance, trouble between Henry de Trafford and William Hackyng and Christiana his wife prior to 1278. This concerned seven dwellings, eight oxgangs of land, two acres of meadow and 10s rent in Stretford, Chorlton and Withington. All this had been held by William and Christiana who was, asserts Crofton[20], the widow of Richard de Trafford and whose dower this property was. Henry (probably the son of Richard de Trafford) claimed the property as his inheritance and on 20th January 1278 an agreement between the parties resulted in William and Christiana accepting Henry's right. Henry on his part recognized the release by giving them, as a token, one sor sparrowhawk.[21]

A deed executed about 1280 between Sir Simon de Gousil and Henry de Trafford is endorsed to the effect that tenants in Chorlton[22] were required to grind their corn at their lord's mill at Didsbury. 'Sir Simon de Gousil, knight, releases &c to Henry de Trafford his heirs and assigns the homage of the said Henry and his heirs, together with the several annual rents which the said Henry owes for all the lands he holds of him in divers places within the fee of Withington. He releases, moreover, and quit-claims to the said Henry &c. the suit payable by his Chorlton tenants, in respect of his mill at Didsbury, all services, exactions, &c., of what nature soever, to which the said Henry might be liable, the said Henry rendering homage therefor to the chief lord of Manchester, and paying him yearly at the feast of St. Michael one pair of gloves and one penny.' Witnessed by D'ne Galfr'o de Bracebrigg, Galfr. de Chaderton, Ric'o de Radeclive, Ric'o de Moston, Rob'to de Shorisworth, Jordano de Crompton and others.

THE BARLOW FAMILY (I)

The Barlow family is first noted about 1300 when there is a reference to Sir Robert Barlow (A) having a mill on the Mersey as part of the manor—by which is probably meant the estate. This error creeps in frequently but although there is nothing whatever to suggest that the Barlow estates were ever anything other than a part of the manor of Withington, the Barlows certainly seem to have enjoyed a sort of extra-manorial position with a large measure of freedom. In 1600 Rowland Mosley brought a suit against Sir Alexander Barlow in which he stated that the Barlow estate was held by 'Knightes service and by a certayne yearlye Rente as a Charterer and freeholder of the . . . Mannor of Withington'.

Note: In order to make it easier to follow the descent of the Barlow and Moseley/Mosley families, each member has been given a letter which is indicated behind the name in the text and corresponds to the same individual in the family trees.

It is possible that the mill referred to is that at Didsbury: Alexander, capellanus (minister) of Didsbury conveys to

'. . . Roger de Barlow the elder (C) all his lands in Barlow, Chollerton, Harday in Withington, together with a water mill there situated with remainder to Thomas (G), son of Roger de Barlow (C) and Marion his wife. . . .'[23]

but there is this suggestion that the Barlow family mill was at Harday, not Didsbury, which one would expect to be mentioned if it were that one.

In an estate map of the Egertons concerned with the drainage of the Barlow Estate in 1804, the river banks shown are such that taken in association with the water courses marked, the name of 'Mill Field' for the adjacent land and the position relative to the Hall and the 'Home Farm' (Barlow Hall Farm) as to leave little doubt as to the probability that there was a mill sited here (818919) at some period. In 1429–30, Sir Edmund de Trafford bore witness respecting a weir on the Mersey situated near the site of the later 'Jackson's Boat'.[24] The position of the supposed mill would satisfactorily conform to this position and a weir across the river would be an essential part of the installation.

Sir Robert de Barlow (A) lived in Barlow Hall in the reign of Edward I (1272–1307). There is no definite knowledge of the family residing here before that date. Sir Montague Barlow Bt. ('Barlow Family Records', p. 28 et seq. (published privately?) c. 1932) refers to a memorandum prepared by Randle Holmes, the Chester antiquary, in 1653 containing an abstract of the deeds in the muniment room at Barlow Hall. From this he deduces that there were family links with Derbyshire through Ughtred (or Uchtred) who, seemingly, held land in both Lancashire and at Barleie (i.e. Barlow) near Chesterfield and not very far from Barlborough, Longford and Hathersage. Sir Montague suggests that the ancient Norman family of D'Abitot, who had settled at Barleie and were, by the time of Edward I, dropping the clan title of D'Abitot, intermarried with the Hathersages, de Longfords and Gresleys. The home of the latter family (Gresley near Burton on Trent) is hard by Seale (i.e. Sale) which was tenanted by the Albini family who also held land in Salford Hundred. From this it is sensible to conclude that just as the Gresleys (a branch of the Albinis), the Hathersages and the Longfords were sending their younger sons to settle on Mersey-side, a de Barlow came too. Alexander, son of Albini of Seale, settled all his lands in Barlow on Thomas de Barlow (B) for the service of two pairs of white gloves at Christmas; Geoffrey de Chetham led the witnesses to the deed and Richard de Trafford, William de Heton, William de Diddesbury and Richard de Chollerton supported him.

Assuming that this theorising is correct, it should be noted that the arms of the Barlows of Lancashire show no resemblance to other Barlow family arms but a similar one occurs in the Albini family and it was not unusual for a newly established family to adopt the arms of their feudal lord, differencing them by such means as a colour switch or reversal of elements.

Whitaker attributes the name to Boarlow or 'boar-ground' but the Oxford Dictionary quotes O. E. Berehlaw 'Barley-hill'. In the light of the foregoing the name would seem to be an imported one, whatever its etymology. Amongst several undated deeds of this period relating to the Barlows is one by which Sybil, daughter of Ughtred (probably the one already mentioned), and his wife Margaret, gave all her lands in Barlow to Thomas de Barlow (B). This may well have been to regularise the transfer of her dowry, indicating that she was the wife of Thomas. The witnesses are Richard de Trafford, Hugh de Trafford, Hugh de Stretford with Sir Geoffrey de Chetham in the lead—as he so often was.

A deed which refers to the Barlows of Barlow but which can-not be fitted into the family tree is recorded for 1311 where Henry, son of Alexander de Barlow gave lands &c. in the town of Withinton (*sic*) to William de Honford. Geoffrey de Chetham (who was at this time seneschal of Manchester, i.e. the steward to the lord), Hugh de Phitun (Fitton?), Richard de Trafford and Robert de Redish were the witnesses.[25] In 1466 Nicholas

Barlow (M) conveyed to his son Alexander (N) lands in Withington so, obviously, all the family holdings in that town had not been passed to William de Honford.

Another confusing deed is that, undated, by which Amicia, daughter of Roger de Barlow, gives to Roger (C), son of Thomas de Barlow (B), the half bovate of land in Barlow which her father gave her on her marriage.[26] Amicia, who married Hamo (Humphrey) de Barlow (!) was Roger's aunt.

In 1336 (Edward III), Roger de Barlow the elder (C), as querent (plaintiff) and Robert de Cattelow, deforcient (one who withholds possession from its rightful owner) were parties to an action at York. The action concerned the manor (estate?) of Barlow, five messuages, fifty acres of land, six acres of meadow, with their appurtenances in Chollerton and half the manor (township?) of Chollerton &c. The deed there issued confirms to

'. . . the said Roger (C) the possession of the lands in question for his life, with remainder to Roger his son (E) and Agnes his son's wife (F), and his heirs male, with remainder to Thurstan, brother of the aforesaid Henry with remainder to Thomas (G), son of Roger de Barlow the elder (C), with remainder to the right heirs of the said Roger Barlow the elder (C). . . .'

Thurstan and Henry were brothers of Roger (E). A certificate issued at Lichfield in 1397 (the parish of Manchester was then in the diocese of Lichfield) asserts that Thomas de Barlow (B) was the sole and exclusive lord of Barlow, that his father's name was Robert de Barlow (A), that Thomas had two sons of whom the elder was Roger (C) and the younger Thomas (D); that Roger (C) in his time became sole lord of Barlow and that he had a son Roger (E), who succeeded his father as lord of Barlow. There were three Rogers in a line of which the youngest Roger (H) and his wife Ellen bought fourteen acres of land from Thomas de Bruche in 1341 for ten marks.

Robert Collayn in 1390 gave to John (J) the son of Roger de Barlow (H) for the term of his life all his messuages, lands, &c. in Barlow, Chollerton, &c., with remainder to John (K), son of John (J) and the heirs of the body of John (K) the younger and Joan the daughter of Richard de Holland.[27] John Barlow the younger was one of those 'summoned by the bell' to

Manchester in 1422 to accord consent to the plan of Thomas de la Warre, lord of the Manor and rector of the Parish Church, to found a college and establish the Parish Church of St. Mary as a collegiate church.

Nicholas Barlow (M) entered into a marriage-covenant in 1434 with Richard de Ashton de Mersey Bank (i.e. Ashton on Mersey) for the marriage of his son Alexander (N) to Elizabeth, daughter of Richard. This same Nicholas (M) and his son Alexander (N) in 1450 leased to George Barlow a close (field) in Barlow for a period of four years and on 3rd December 1466 Nicholas (M) conveyed to Alexander (N) all his lands in Withington and elsewhere in Lancashire which he had inherited from his father John (K).

For some reason not specified, but probably to safeguard his son's inheritance, Alexander (N) conveyed his estate on trust to John Radcliffe of Radcliffe, Esq., Thurstan Tildesley, Esq., James Hill, rector of Northenden and Ralph Ashton, rector of Ashton. Roger (O) was the son of Alexander and he married Catherine, daughter of Ellis Prestwich of Hulme. The estate had returned to him because on his death it passed to Ellis Barlow whose christian name was that of his grandfather on his mother's side.

Roger and his wife are recorded as having three children. Ellis (P), already mentioned, married Anne, a daughter of Otes Reddish of Reddish and through Ellis the estate was transmitted. The two other children were Elizabeth who married Nicholas Eyre of Hope in Derbyshire and Edmund who married twice; in the first instance to a daughter, name unrecorded, of a Mr. Jackson of Manchester and in the second to Anne the daughter of Sir Piers Dutton of Dutton and widow of Hamnet Massey of Sale. This seems to be a convenient point at which to leave the Barlow family for the time being.

TOWARDS A CHURCH OF ITS OWN

An interesting sidelight on the way in which ownership could be far removed from residence is that of Elias Entwisell of Entwissel Manor, near Bolton, who is recorded in the rent-roll of Thomas de la Warre, 1473, as holding one messuage with appurtenances in Chorleton in soccage[28] and by a yearly rent of 3s 4d. Edmund Entwissel held this at his death in 1544 and in 1576 it was the subject of litigation between Edward Tildesley and Alexander Entwysell.[12]

Until the early years of the XIII century the people of the township had to travel to the parish church of Manchester for baptisms, weddings and burials so it is unlikely that they would otherwise attend very frequently. According to where they lived they would make their way down the 'Back Lane' (Hawthorn Lane of later years and sometime known as Briscatt Lane) or along the Edge Lane and then by the old Roman road; or past the 'Flash' and down Trafford Lane (or Chorlton Lane if you lived at the other end, and now known as Seymour Grove) to join the road at Trafford; or by way of White Moss, through the lord's demesne[29] and Moss Side. Their occasional spiritual needs would be satisfied by priests from Manchester who would hold services as and where the opportunity presented itself. No doubt the problems of wresting a living were such that strict religious observance came second in their life.

About 1235 Didsbury Chapel was built:

'William, chaplain of Dedesbury came not on the first day; so fined.'

is recorded in the Lancashire Assize Roll of 1246. Though probably built as a private chapel it seems to have soon extended its availability to others until it became a parochial chapel. In 1352 Roger de Norbury, Bishop of Lichfield, granted a commission for the chapel yard to be consecrated in order that those who died of the plague in Didsbury and the neighbourhood could be buried there in view of the distance from Manchester.[30]

This would relieve Chorltonians, at least those on the Didsbury side, of a considerable journey. Their probable route would lie across the ford at Chorlton Brook (Brook-road Bridge) through Hardy and along a path which was roughly parallel to Darley Avenue. This path existed until the building of the housing estate and the right of way is still perpetuated in the path from Chorltonville to Hurstville Road.

Before 1413 the chapel at Stretford was built. The inhabitants of the township living in Chorlton and Martledge now had a place of worship even more convenient than Didsbury. As time moved on, particularly after the separation of Hough End from the township, Chorlton tended to be associated more and more with Stretford and had not it been within the Manor of Withington and therefore associated with the Withington Urban District Council on its formation, it may well have now been a part of the Borough of Stretford rather than the City of Manchester.

The road pattern changed but little in the middle ages. Access to the fields lying away from the few roads was by path or occupation roads. The nearest main road was still in the Watling-street and even after a thousand years of use with no maintenance it was superior to other more recent tracks. The importance of salt in the lives of people led to the bestowing of the name 'saltways' on other roads which were brought into existence as much to facilitate general trade as to distribute salt. Such a road cut through Northenden, across the Mersey at the ford at Didsbury and so into south-east Lancashire and York-shire. These two 'main' roads were the nearest that the traveller came to Chorlton and so it and its people were left undisturbed and free from many of the ills which contact with the outside world brought in its wake.

The banks of the river have already been mentioned as pos-sibly originating in the pre-Conquest era, and certainly by the middle ages there were considerable banks in existence to try to control the river and force it to scour its own course. Refer-ence to the 1845 map will show that there are three places along the township boundary where the line trespasses on the wrong side of the river. These deviations probably arise from gradual changes in course by the natural action of the river itself coupled with a measure of control by man; but that at 'Jack-son's Boat', by far the best known instance since it is associated with the pub being in Lancashire but on the Cheshire side of the river, presents an intriguing possibility. If we remember the matter of the Barlow mill, which was a short distance upstream from the start of this deviation and the fact that water mills usually have a 'tail' island which extends some distance down-stream, separating the race from the river, we are within the realms of reasonable possibility as seeing this as yet another piece of evidence for the existence of the mill. Circumstantial, certainly, but it is easy to see that the present course of the river may have developed from the old mill race, faster flowing and on the Barlow side of the river, while the slower main stream, now silted up, had its course where the boundary line is.

Those who tilled the fields in those past ages were well aware of the need to control the flood waters in the ees and of the benefit of the layer of rich silt left by the receding water. Within the memory of people still alive the farmer who last tenanted Barlow Hall Farm commented that the sluice gates in the banks were never opened for the first flood of the year for this brought down the rubbish, but the second flood brought down the rich mud.

The end of the XV century is a convenient point to end the second phase in Chorlton's story.

NOTES

[10] Harleian MSS. 2077 fol. 292, referring to the de Trafford family makes various statements, of which:
'Note before yᵉ Conquest the Gentry and Nobility were called of theire place and habitaͨon; yᵉ vulgar Sorte had noe Sirnames but called of their trades as brewer baker wright or of some defecte of body as wild lame &c.'

[11] See 'A History of Didsbury' by Ivor R. Million for fuller details of the Longford family.

[12] Booker in 'Ancient Chapels of Didsbury and Chorlton' is responsible for the erroneous and oft quoted '. . . earliest record of landed proprietors. . . .' The wording of the deed is '. . . tͬe meoe in Chorlton scil Bexwic' in pura . . .' which clearly intends '. . . in a certain part of Chorlton namely Beswick. . .' and must therefore refer to Chorlton Row. References hereafter to Chorlton so far as the de Chorltons, the de Traffords, and where the Manor of Manchester is mentioned should be accepted with care.

[13] Radulphi, the earliest of the de Traffords, is considered to have lived at the time of King Canute, 1017-42.

[14] Booker H.C.D.C. p. 245.

[15] Harleian MSS. fol. 137.

[16] An instrument whereby the owner of legal title to property could claim possession from a tenant.

[17] Harleian MSS. 2085, fol. 528.

[18] Booker H.C.D.C., p. 242.

[19] Booker H.C.D.C., p. 242/3.

[20] Crofton H.S.C., III p. 179.

[21] Sor (+age)—a first-year bird, a young bird.

[22] 'Tenants of Chollerton owe a rent to Didsbury Milne.' refers to Chorlton-cum-Hardy as evidence proves that the tenants of Chorlton Row were required to use the mill at Manchester.

[23] Harleian MSS. 2112, fol. 172.

[24] Crofton H.S.C. III, p. 228.

[25] Harleian MSS. 2112, fol. 165.

[26] Booker H.C.D.C., p. 249.

[27] Harleian MSS. 2112, fol. 173. Witnessed by John de Radcliffe de Chaderton, Adam de Lever jnr., Richard de Redish, James de Barlow. Joan (L) was probably the wife of John the Younger (K).

[28] Socage—tenure by defined services distinct from military tenure and villainage.

[29] c.f. Demesne Road. The demesne was the part of a manor retained by the lord as his own.

[30] Hollingworth. The Black Death had visited Manchester in 1350.

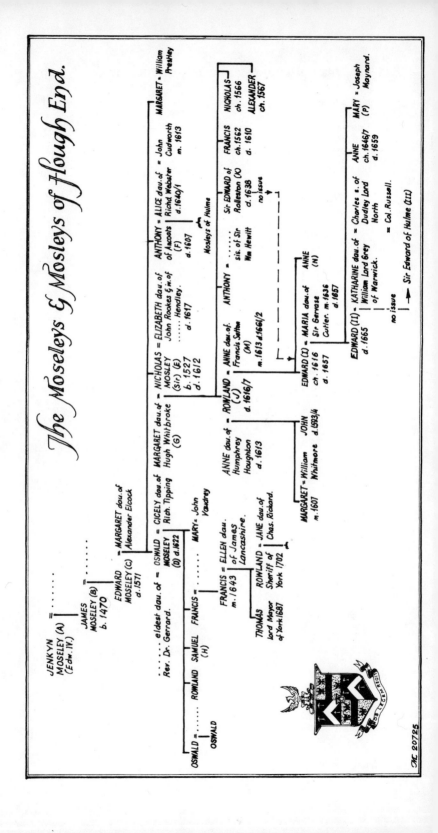

The Moseleys & Moseleys of Hough End.

JENKYN MOSELEY (A) (Edw. IV.) = ...

JAMES MOSELEY (B) b. 1470 = ...

EDWARD MOSELEY (C) d. 1571 = MARGARET dau. of Alexander Elcock

OSWALD MOSELEY (D) d. 1622 = CICELY dau. of Rich. Tipping

MARGARET dau. of Hugh Whitbroke (G) = NICHOLAS MOSELEY (Sir) (E) b. 1527 d. 1612 = ELIZABETH dau. of John Rookes & w. of ...... Hendley. d. 1617

ANTHONY of Ancoats (F) d. 1607 = ALICE dau. of Richd. Webster. d. 1640/1 = John Cudworth m. 1613

MARGARET = William Prestley

Moseleys of Hulme

.... eldest dau. of Rev. Dr. Gerrard. = OSWALD = MARY = John Vawdrey

OSWALD = ...

ROWLAND   SAMUEL   FRANCIS (H)

FRANCIS = ELLEN dau. of James Lancashire. m. 1643

THOMAS Lord Mayor of York 1687

ROWLAND Sheriff of York 1702 = JANE dau. of Chas. Rickard.

ANNE dau. of Humphrey Houghton d. 1613 = ROWLAND (J) d. 1616/7

ANTHONY = ... sis. of Sir Wm Hewitt

FRANCIS ch. 1562 d. 1610   NICHOLAS ch. 1566   ALEXANDER ch. 1567

Sir EDWARD of Rolleston (K) d. 1638   no issue

MARGARET = William Whitmore m. 1607

JOHN d. 1593/4

EDWARD (I) ch. 1616 d. 1657 = MARIA dau. of Sir Gervase Cutler. m. 1636 d. 1657

ANNE dau. of Francis Sutton (M) m. 1613 d. 1661/2

ANNE (N)

EDWARD (II) d. 1665 = KATHARINE dau. of William Lord Grey of Warwick.   no issue

Charles s. of Dudley Lord North   = Col. Russell.

ANNE ch. 1646/7 d. 1659

MARY ch. 1646/7 (P) = Joseph Maynard.

⟶ Sir Edward of Hulme (III)

HC 20725

The Chorlton 'bus at the Flash (West Point) c. 1905. The vehicle is in Manchester Tramways livery and the scene is obviously posed. (source unknown).

The electric tram from Brooks's Bar and Belle Vue penetrates the boundary at West Point about 1905, at least the nearer line is in Chorlton, the far one is in Stretford! The wall on the left, where shops now are, was the wall of Darley Hall. (comm. p.c.).

Edge Lane looking from Highfield Rd. (now Kingshill Road) towards High Lane. c. 1907. The 'bus belonged to the Manchester District Motor Omnibus Co. of whose services little is known. (comm. p.c.).

Lane End, when it was the tram terminus, prob. c. 1910 (Neil's Series).

The 'Tram Terminus c. 1917. (Bax's grocers shop bears an invitation to register for all rationed goods.) (source unknown).

A sunny afternoon outside Southern Cemetery gates, June 1915. (coll. R. Dunning).

Exterior of Chorlton Station, c. 1890. (comm. p.c. ref. L 5009).

Manchester Central - Guide Bridge train approaching Chorlton Junction, 1950 (photo. H. Duck).

Chapter Three

The opening of the XVI century marked the commencement of a period of great change. The Moseley family, from Staffordshire, took up local residence and became lords of the Manors of Manchester and Withington; the Barlows entered into a period of persecution for their religious beliefs and Chorlton at last achieved a chapel of its own.

THE MOSELEYS AND MOSLEYS

The first reference to the family of Moseley is recorded in the family memoirs, printed and published by Sir Oswald Mosley for private circulation in 1849. Therein it is stated that the family originated in the district of Moseley near Wolverhampton, the surname developing in the usual manner from 'de Moseley'. In Anglo-Saxon, meos = a moss and leay = a field (c.f. 'ley' as in Barlow-ley).

A Saxon, Ernald, held lands in the reign of King John; he had two sons of which the eldest, William, died without male issue and three daughters, of which Juliana married a John de Bilston who, with the estates at Moseley so acquired, adopted the name of Moseley.

The second son was Oswald or Osbert and his children migrated to Lancashire and Yorkshire and from this branch of the family we find Robert Moseley holding a burgage near the bridge in Manchester in the thirteenth year of the reign of Edward IV (1473).

Jenkyn Moseley of Withington, Gent., lived at Hough End in 1465 and married an heiress of whom nothing is known, not even her name, other than that her family arms were 'or, a fess sable, between three eaglets displayed sable.'[31] He quartered his arms with hers and had it recognized by the Heralds.[32]

Jenkyn (A) was succeeded by James (B) who was born in 1469, and was succeeded in turn by Edward (C) who married Margaret, daughter of Alexander Elcocke of Stockport. Edward died in 1571 and left three sons: Oswald (D), Nicholas (E) and Anthony (F) and one daughter, Margaret.

Oswald established himself in Manchester as a clothier and

purchased Garratt Hall (on the bank of the Medlock where Princess Street passes under the M.S.J. Railway and roughly on the same site as the public house of similar name). He took an active part in local affairs and was misegatherer (tax collector) in 1589, constable in 1590, affeeror (assessor of taxes and fines) in 1591 and overseer of the conduit in 1595.

He was married twice, firstly to the eldest daughter of the Rev. Dr. Gerrard, rector of Stockport, from which marriage there appears to have been no issue, and secondly to Cicely, the daughter of Richard Tipping of Manchester. His second marriage produced four sons and one daughter, of which the third son, Samuel (H), inherited his father's estate, sold it, and went to Ireland. Oswald died at Garratt Hall in 1622.

Margaret, the only daughter of Edward, married William Prestly of London, which leaves us to consider Nicholas (E) and Anthony (F) by whom the fortunes of the family were to be founded.

This was a period of intense commercial expansion and anybody who could put a sum of money at risk was engaged in buying and selling. Particularly was this commercial endeavour concerned with wool textiles for English wool was in demand all over Europe and the near-East. The pantomime story of Dick Whittington is a very fair representation of the way in which fortunes were made.

Nicholas and Anthony embarked in trade in Manchester, probably buying fleeces from small-holders at shearing time and distributing them to cottage weavers who were paid for their work and the cloth so produced sold at a profit at the fairs and markets of the district. No doubt it soon became obvious to the two brothers that a little organization would provide an even greater return on their outlay, and so it was decided that Anthony should organize the local end of the venture and Nicholas should go to London where he could profitably arrange the export of the cloth.

Anthony purchased the Ancoats estate of Sir John Byrom and was married to Alice, daughter of Richard Webster of Manchester. They had many children and reference to this branch of the family will be made later. Anthony died 25th March 1607, Alice survived him and married John Cudworth of Werneth at the Collegiate Church on 3rd May 1613.

Nicholas, in London, prospered. His business associations inevitably brought him in contact with politics and before 1590 he was an alderman of the Aldersgate Ward of the City. In that year of 1590 he served in the office of Sheriff. An aldermanship of Langbourn Ward followed in 1594 and he achieved the ultimate office of Lord Mayor in 1599. This highest rank, as fortune had it, was his opportunity to demonstrate his capabilities to the full, for this was a time of fear lest Spain should launch an attack on the country in retaliation for the defeat of the 'Invincible Armada' of 1588. London was responsible for providing Elizabeth I with 6,000 soldiers and 16 warships as well as strengthening the defences of the City against attack. As if this was not enough there were fears of insurrection in Ireland and a demand for 500 men and several ships on this account had also to be met. The realisation of these considerable targets was energetically pursued by the Lord Mayor and was so successful that the Queen indicated her approval by bestowing on him a knighthood and, as a more tangible symbol, several articles of furniture, including a handsome carved oak bedstead, for his recently-erected house at Hough End.

The original manor house of Withington was 'the Hough', an ancient building thought to be in the half timbered style (it is unlikely to have been otherwise) and surrounded by a moat. This building, known as the 'Old Hall', survived until about the mid-XVIII century when it was demolished to make way for a farmhouse which went by the name of 'Chorlton's' or 'Old Hall' Farm. The moat remained in part until the Old Moat housing estate was built and is now recorded by a tablet stating that the houses to which it is affixed, standing in Eddisbury Avenue, are on the site of the old manor house of Withington (ref. 840935). It has been stated that this was the home of Jenkyn Moseley in 1465 which would raise the question of where the Longfords, as lords of the Manor, lived at this time. Although evidence infers that they latterly lived at Longford in Derbyshire[33] and their visits to Withington infrequent, it is unlikely that this was Jenkyn Moseley's home.

The Family Memoirs indicate that the present Hough End Hall was built on the same site as an earlier house. Booker (no doubt basing his comment on the Memoirs) states:

'. . . for the new house which he had recently erected at

Hough End on the site of the old mansion, the seat of his ancestors.'[34]

In the will of Nicholas it is pointed out:

'Also whereas I heretofore dyd take a lease of Mr Langford of the house and grounde wherein I dwell for three score and tenne yéares whereof there bee div'rs yeares yett unexpyred. . . .'

As the present house was built in 1596 and Sir Nicholas was 85 on his death in 1612, it would seem that the lease must have been entered into many years before and referred to the earlier building. Possibly it dated from the death of his father in 1571.

Nicholas was married twice. His first wife was Margaret (G), daughter of Hugh Whitbroke of Bridgenorth (*sic*) in Shropshire.[35] The date of the marriage is not known but from it there were six children: Rowland (J) the eldest and successor, Anthony, Francis, Nicholas, Alexander and Edward (K), the latter 'taking to the Law'.

On receiving his knighthood Nicholas would accept a grant of arms and, as customary, a motto which in the fashion of the times was a punning one: MOS LEGEM REGIT—Custom (or precedent) rules the law. To make it more perfect he changed the spelling of the family name from Moseley to Mosley. Booker states '. . . it is stated in compliment to his son Edward, then rising into note as a barrister.' though it would seem more probable that it was the choice of motto which paid compliment to Edward.

Margaret his first wife died and in 1592 he married Elizabeth, the daughter of John Rookes and widow of — Hendley of London who survived him. In 1596, whilst in London, he purchased the Manor of Manchester from John Lacy of London, an action probably designed to invest some part of his fortune in safety since banks, as we know them, did not then exist. Lacy, also a cloth merchant, had bought the Manor from the West's in 1579 for £3,000 and sold it to Sir Nicholas for £3,500. A fair return in seventeen years!

In 1604 he was appointed High Sheriff of the County of Lancaster, an office which was later to be held for a brief period by his eldest son Rowland.

The 'laste Will and Testam'.' of Sir Nicholas is a quite remarkable document revealing the pains taken with details.[36]

An approximate count gives roughly 3,750 words which cover everything one would think of and many that one would not. Provision is made for his widow:

'. . . that is to saie, ffirst my will and mynde is that Dame Elizabeth nowe my wief shall have soe muche, if shee bee contented therewith, as my sonne Rowland (J) and myself have covenanted to paye her yearlie, wch is the sōme of three hundred poundes ev'rie yeare duringe her n'rall lief, and the sōme of xxx^li [37] a yeare more to be payde duringe her widowhood for her house rente, . . .'

The possessions of Elizabeth which had become her husband's on her marriage were returned to her:

'Also I give and bequeath to my said wief in lieu of her chamber two of my beste beddes wth the furniture accordinglie, excepte the beste tapestrie cov'ringe and the beste bedstocke alsoe excepted. Also I give and bequeath unto my said wief all such plate as shee had att the tyme I married her, save onlie one pott wch was stoolene awaye in the tyme of my mayroltie in London. And also I give and bequeath unto my said wief her chaine and braslett and her wearinge apparell and all things hereunto belonginge.'

Coache, coache-horses, furniture, lynnens, all in turn were conveyed . . .

'. . . butt if my said wief bee not therew^th contented butt shall in anie wise sue and trouble my executo^r or his assignes for anie furth^r or oth^r portions, that then my will and mynde is that my former guiftes and bequeathes shall cease and be utterlie voyde. . . .'

Having provided for his wife, he turned to other bequests:

'. . . I give to a schoolem^r to teache scoole att Chollerton Chapell five poundes ev'ie yeare duringe twentie yeares next after my decease oute of my rentes of the Denorie of Bridge North (i.e. Bridgnorth, Shropshire), yearlie to be receaved; Provided alwaies that my two sonnes Rowland Mosley and Edward Mosley and my nephew Oswolde Mosley (L) sonne to my late broth^r Anthonie Mosley (F) or anie two of them, theire heires or assignes, shall have the nominacōn of the said schoolem^r; and provided alsoe that the said scholem^r shall not take of anie scholler above vj^d a quarter of a yeares teacheinge; and alsoe that my two sonnes and my said nephewe or anie two of them, theire heires or assignes shall have power to discharge the said schoolem^r if hee bee negligent in teacheinge his schollers, ...

The payment to the schoolmaster was to be:

'. . . payde att the feaste of St. Michaell th' arkangle and the annunciacon of the blessed Virgin Marie by equall p'cōns or wthin fourtie daies of eith^r of the said feastes nexte ensueinge. . . .'

The schollmaster was expected to give value for money for he was required to:

'. . . reade praire three tymes ev'ie week in the said chapell.'

A sum of five pounds or more a year 'mayntenance wch Mr Chorleton gave the said scoole . . . .' was to be employed as directed by Mr. Chorleton, which suggests that Nicholas feared some dishonesty somewhere.

Edward (the one who had taken to the Law) seems to have purchased Alport Lodge and a part of Alport Park.[38] The will provided for Nicholas, or his executor, to pay Edward £950 for the transfer of the property to Rowland within one year. This instruction was satisfied for there was a threat written into the will that if the payment was not made the manors or lordships of Prestall Lee and Walkden were to go to Edward. The property played a part in the Siege of Manchester. Rowland, as the eldest son would expect, received the Manor of Manchester and

'. . . the mann^{rs} and lordshipps of Houghe, Withington and Didsburie and all and ev'rie the lands . . . etc . . . and hereditam^{ts} in Houghe, Withington, Didsburie, Burnedge, Eaton Wood green, ffallowefeild, Houghend, Yealdhouse, Moss-greane, Ladiebarne, Rushoolme, Barscrofte, Chorleton, Chollerton, Streford, Turvemosse, Lydle heath and Birchall houses. . . .'[39]

Rowland is quoted by some authorities as having purchased the manor of Withington in 1597 (the actual date being 13th December). This was while his father was active in London and the continuation of the above extract:

'. . . in as large and ample mann^r as they be stated and conveyed unto him by one deede of Intayle bearinge date

the xxviij[th] daie of July inste in the fourth yeare of the raigne of the Kinges Ma[tie] that nowe is as oth[r] waies.'
suggests that he had bought it on behalf of his father and not in his own right. The date of the deed of entail would be 1607.

Edward received various properties, particularly certain houses and tenements which his father had bought from Stephen Browne and Alexander Sorocoulde.

Rowland was the executor and:

'. . . my lovinge nephewes Oswell Mosley and ffrancis Mosley . . . and my cosins Jacob Procter and Alexander Elcock. . . .'

supervisors for which they were to receive l[s] (that is 50 sh. not one shilling)

'. . . a peece' to make ev'rie one of them a ringe to weare for my sake.'

The will was witnessed by Robert Gee, Robert Barlow, Lawrence Crowder and Will[m] Harrison.

Dame Elizabeth seems not to have had any quarrel with the will and she survived her husband by about five years, dying in 1617. She was buried with her husband in Didsbury chapel. Her will[40] is scarcely less embracing than that of her husband, though she strikes a rather different note in specifying that her funeral was to be:

'. . . in the day tyme and in the company of neighboures and not privilie nor in the night tyme.'

Her executors were instructed to:

'lay forth one hundred and three score pounds in or about my funerall, or more if they in their owne discrecōns shall think it fittinge. . . .'

The figure intended would be £160, a goodly sum in those days, rather than the £2060 which could be inferred.

The poor of Manchester were to receive £10, and of the 'Lord-shippe of the Houghe, Chollerton and Heaton Norres' £10. £5 was for the bewtifying of Diddisbury Chappell. Among the very many small bequests was ten shillings to Robert Hulme at the 'Chappel style in Chollerton'. Elizabeth must have been a kindly soul for she left

'. . . to Anne Whitmore, daughter of William Whitmore of London esquier five markes to buy some pretie jewell to weare for a remembrance from me.'

Step-son Edward (K) and cosen Oswald (L) (really he was her nephew) were to be executors, receiving £10 each for their pains, and William Sparke and Robert Barlowe were overseers, receiving £10 each.

The inventory of goods and chattels of Dame Elizabeth were valued, 24th May 1617, at £1,259 16s 3d, and included:

Imp.	Best bedd and ffurniture, excepte bed-stockes	xij^{li}		
It.	One scarlet petticoate wth three gardes of velvet	ij^{li}	x^{s}	
It.	One scarlet petticoate wth twoe gardes of velvet	ij^{li}		
It.	One oulde scarlet petticoate ..		xxx^{s}	
It.	One crimson sattin petticoate ..	v^{li}		
It.	One damask petticoate ymbroidered	v^{li}		
It.	One velvett hudd..		xx^{s}	
It.	An oulde gowne, a kirtle, a remnante of grogran and twoe yeardes of scyprus	iiij^{li}		
It.	Halfe the rest of the lynnen praised	xxviij^{li}	xij^{s}	
It.	One paire of bracelettes of gould	x^{li}		
It.	Twoe silver cannes, percell guilte	vj^{li}	xiij^{s} iiij^{d}	
It.	A broken ffanne		x^{s}	
It.	An old coache and twoe coache horses	vij^{li}		
It.	One goulde cheane 21 oz. & $\frac{3}{4}$ at 1v^{s} oz.	lx^{li}		
It.	Three tuns, one great salte wth a cover, a trencher salt, a standing salt, three boules, twoe dozen spoones, twoe cannes, one broken boule and broken silver—all waying 174 oz. $\frac{3}{4}$ at v^{s} the oz.	xliij^{li}	xiij^{s} ix^{d}	

Sir Nicholas had six sons by Margaret his first wife. Rowland the heir to the estates and Edward the third son are the two most concerned with the family story. The second son was Anthony who married the sister of Sir William Hewett and

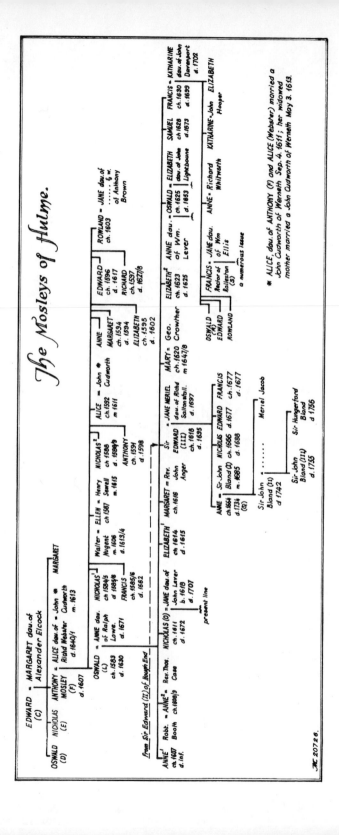

The Mosleys of Hulme.

EDWARD = MARGARET dau.of
(C)   Alexander Elcock

OSWALD   NICHOLAS   ANTHONY = ALICE dau.of = John *   MARGARET
(D)   (E)   MOSLEY   Richd Webster   Cudworth
                      (F)   m. 1613
                      d. 1640/1

OSWALD = ANNE dau.   Walter = ELLEN = Henry   NICHOLAS² = ALICE = John *   ANNE   EDWARD = JANE dau.of   ROWLAND = JANE dau.of
(L)   of Ralph   Nugent   ch.1587 Sewell   ch.1586   ch.1592 Cudworth   ch.1596   Richard   ch.1603   ...... & w.
ch.1583 Lowe.   m.1606   m.1615   d.1589/9   m.1611   MARGARET   d. 1617   of Anthony
d. 1630   d.1613/4   ANTHONY   ch.1594   RICHARD   Brown
         FRANCIS   ch.1591   d. 1594   ch.1597
         ch.1585/6   d. 1598   ELIZABETH d.1627/8
         d. 1662   ch.1595
                                                                             d. 1602

From Sir Edward (II) of Booth End

ELIZABETH¹ = Rev.   MARGARET = Rev.   Sir   MARY = Geo.   ELIZABETH² = OSWALD = ELIZABETH   SAMUEL   FRANCIS = KATHARINE
ch.1614   Geo.   ch.1616   John   EDWARD   ch.1620 Crowther ch.1623   ch.1625 dau. of John ch.1628 ch.1630 dau.of John
d. 1615   Crowther   Anger (III)   m 1647/8   d. 1625   Lightbourne   d.1673 d.1699   Davenport
                                         ch.1618   d. 1702
                                         d.1695

NICHOLAS (0) = JANE dau.of
ch.1611   John Lever
d. 1672   b. 1618
              d. 1707

present line

Robt. = ANNE²
Booth   ch.1607
        d. Inf.

Rev.Thos.
Case
ch.1608/9

ANNE¹

= JANE MERIEL
dau.of Richd
Saltonstall.
d. 1697

Sir
EDWARD
(III)
ch.1618
d.1695

ANNE = Sir-John   NICHOLAS EDWARD FRANCIS
ch.1664 Bland(I) ch.1666 ch.1677 ch.1677
d.1734   m.1685   d. 1688 d. 1677 d. 1677
(30)

FRANCIS = JANE dau.
Rector of   of Wm
Rolleston   Ellis
(3)
a numerous issue

OSWALD
(4)
EDWARD
ROWLAND

ANNE = Richard   KATHARINE = John   ELIZABETH
       Whitworth   Hooper

Sir-John = ...   Meriel Jacob
Bland (II)
d 1742

Sir-John   Sir-Hungerford
Bland (III)   Bland
d. 1755   d. 1756

* ALICE, dau. of ANTHONY (F) and ALICE (Webster) married a
  John Cudworth of Werneth Sep. 4. 1611; her widowed
  mother married a John Cudworth of Werneth May 3. 1613.

JE 207726.

whose dissolute habits estranged him from his friends. The other three seem to have pre-deceased their father, certainly Francis died in July 1610, at the age of 48.

Rowland, the oldest son and successor, married Anne, daughter of Humphrey Houghton of Manchester, and was left a widower in 1613 with a daughter Margaret. Their other child, John, had died in February 1593–94. Margaret had married William Whitmore of Appley near Bridgnorth, Shropshire. Within a year of his wife's death Rowland had married again. This time he married Anne the daughter of Francis Sutton of Sutton in the county of Cheshire who was co-heiress of Richard Sutton. From this marriage there was only one son, Edward.

Rowland did not live long to enjoy his inheritance. He was appointed High Sheriff of Lancashire in 1616 and died in that same year.

Rowland's estates passed to his son Edward (I) but in order to see how events developed it is necessary to return to Nicholas's son Edward (K), the brother of Rowland. Baptised at Didsbury Church on 17th October 1569, he entered the law, becoming a barrister of considerable note, Member of Parliament for Preston and His Majesty's Attorney-General for the Duchy of Lancaster. He was knighted in 1614 and bought the Rolleston estate in Staffordshire.[41] He was unmarried and on his death in 1638 his property passed to his nephew Edward (I), the son of Rowland.

Edward (I), born in 1616, was only a few months old when his father died; growing up without parental discipline he seems to have developed rather wayward habits and it seems to have been considered expedient to arrange a marriage to Maria, daughter of Sir Gervasse Cutler of Stainborough, Yorkshire, at the youthful age of 20. The marriage took place by license (dated 6th November) in Chorlton Chapel, 15th November 1636. He was a staunch supporter of Charles I who granted a patent of baronetcy to him in 1640. In 1642 he was appointed High Sheriff of Stafford. His adherence to the Royalist cause in the Civil War caused his impoverishment. In 1642 when Manchester, a town of largely Parliamentary sympathies, decided to resist the demands of the Royalists for the handing over of the gunpowder stored in the old college, so precipitating the first clash of the Civil War, Edward put Alport Lodge at the disposal of Lord Strange. The house was burned to the ground during the Siege and the property generally was greatly damaged. The King made frequent demands of his adherents for money with which to fight the war and Edward was forced to turn to Humphrey Chetham from whom he borrowed at eight per cent interest (a high rate for those days) and also from a Mr. Allestrye.

The original loan was for one year and the bond guaranteeing the repayment was dated 20th August 1641. Mr. Chetham did not press for repayment at the end of the stipulated period (being probably well content with the rate of interest and security) and it was not until Trinity Term 1649 that he success-fully applied to the Court of Common Pleas for a judgment against Sir Edward. In the meantime Edward had followed the expensive incident of Alport Lodge by joining a detachment of Royalist troops in Cheshire led by Sir Thomas Aston and Sir Vincent Corbet. They suffered defeat at the hands of the Parlia-mentarians under Sir William Brereton at the Battle of Middle-wich (3rd March 1643) and Edward was taken prisoner.

On his release, having undertaken not to bear arms on behalf of the King, his estates were sequestrated. They were returned to him by an ordinance of Parliament dated 21st September 1647 on payment of a fine of £4,874—a punishment for his de-linquency.

Booker[42] quotes the text of a number of letters exchanged between Anne Mosley, Edward's mother (M), Anne his sister (N), Mr. Allestrye and Humphrey Chetham. Two only are quoted as typical of the spirit of the correspondence. Humphrey Chetham, whatever his good works in other directions, was an exacting money-lender and clearly believed that there is no sentiment in business!

From sister Anne to 'my much hono[rd] friend Humfrey Chetham Esq. att Turton theise present;'

'Worthy S[r],

I thanke you for yo[r] last paynes and kyndnesse and for that greate favo[r] you were then pleased to affoard me in yo[r] patient forbearance of my brother's debt, wherein I was then in good hope you would have received satisfac-čon before this tyme. I understand my brother hath bene lately wth you, and I feare hath bene more free in his pro-

mises than in p'formance. I beseech you give me leave
(beinge imboldened by yo[r] former curtesies) once more to
become an earnest suito[r] to you for a little further forbearance, w[ch] (God willinge) shall not be in any wise
preiudiciall unto you. I am uppon Monday next for my
jorney to London, where I intend to make a finall conclu-
sion for my owne businesse wth S[r] Samuell Sleigh con-
cerninge the money he is to pay me, and shall lykewise (I
hope) putt an end to some thinge betweene my brother and
me, and att my returne from London, which I feare will
be neere Midsomer (if my brother in the meane tyme
satisfye you not) my mother and my selfe will assuredly
(if God blesse us wth lyfe) passe over unto you o[r] intereste
in the Leicestershire landes, w[ch] wee are nowe ascerteyned
from a freind in Leicester are of the fully yearlie value of
seaven hundred poundes or neare thereaboutes. This shall
be my last request unto you in this business, w[ch] if I may
obteyne shall be added to my former ingagem[tes]. Thus for
the p'formance of what I have here undertaken you shall
have that w[ch] I shall ever tenderly p'serve, viz[t] the wordes
and promise of
>Your much obliged freind and servant,
>Anne Mosley.

The enclosed note conteyneth the rent of Beamond Leas
alone, besydes w[ch] wee have in o[r] security Glenfeild
manno[r] and Jelly rowe, w[ch] will make up the yearlie
some I menc̄on in my łre.'

The letter is endorsed by Humphrey 'Mrs. Anne Mosley
łre rec[d] 25 Apr. 1648.'

On 6th October of the same year Humphrey wrote to Miss
Anne Mosley:
>'M[ris] Mosley,
>My tender respect to your reputac̄on especialie and your
ffrends bound wth you, have caused mee att your request
agayne and agayne, ffrom yeare to yeare and from tearme
to tearme, to fforbeare my great some of mony w[ch]
should longe since have beene p[d] me, and wherein I have
undergonne great hasard these troublesome tymes, wherin
I did not doubt but my courtesie would have beene

answered w[th] more correspondent respect ffrom you, an d
especialie that whereas by your last importunetie you
ingaged your selfe w[th] your mother, under both your
hands, that yf I would but fforbeare untill Micklemas now
past, I should w[th]out ffayle have satisfaxiō, w[ch], although
I have continued my patience even to the outemost of
your desier, yet I ffynd noe p'fformance ffrom you. Once
agayne therffore I shall beseech you that you will give mee
no longer cause to suspect your truth and good meaning
towards mee, but doe that w[ch] both the lawe of God and
man requires ffrom you, and w[ch] you may doe w[th]out
p'iudice or detrement to your selfe when you please, and
soe I shall ever rest.

Your ffaythful ffreind and servant,
Humfrey Chetham.

At his successful petition Humphrey Chetham rendered his
account as:

The principall lent 24° August 1641 ..	2000 00 00
Interest for 2000[li] from 24° August 1641 to	
14° Martij 1649, being 8 yeares 6 monthes	
and $\frac{1}{4}$ at 160[li] p ann w[ch] is 13[li] 6[s] 8[d] p	
mensem, amounts to	1366 13 04
Charge of suit	0061 05 00
	3427 17 04
Whereof rec[d] December 1648..	600 00 00
Soe remaines 14° Martij 1649	2827 18 04

(from Booker, p. 148, 3427:17:04 should read 3427:18:04)

Sir Edward agreed that the debt be discharged by a mortgage
on his Leicestershire properties, and, further, that Mr. Allestrye's claim be satisfied from the same source. Both creditors
agreed and accepted Sir Edward's demand for power of redemp-
tion within ten years. The legal arrangements, however, proved
not to be straightforward and finally Mr. Chetham, having
taken counsel's opinion, decided to seek some other source of
repayment. The correspondence between Chetham, Allestrye
and Mrs. and Miss Mosley is incomplete so we cannot say
what the arrangements were for finally discharging the debt.

Sir Edward and his wife Maria had three children. The only son was Edward (II), the two girls being Anne who died in 1659 at the age of 13 and Mary who married Joseph Maynard of Ealing. Sir Edward and his wife both died in 1657 and the estates passed to Edward who was but 17 years of age at the time.

In 1661 Edward came of age, in which year he was returned as Member of Parliament for the St. Michael's division of the county of Cornwall, and obtained an Act of Parliament confirming his purchase of the Hulme estate from the Prestwich family. He married Katharine, daughter of William Lord Grey of Wark and died without issue in 1665. This brought to an end the direct line of descent from Sir Nicholas (E). Katharine married again twice, in the first case to Charles, son and heir to Dudley Lord North and secondly to a Colonel Russell.

It is now necessary to look briefly at the Ancoats branch of the family which stemmed from Anthony (F), the brother of Nicholas. Anthony married Alice, daughter of Richard Webster of Manchester by whom there was a numberous issue. Anthony died at the age of 70 on the 25th March 1607 and his widow, who must have been very much his junior, married John Cudworth of Werneth in 1613. His heir was Oswald (L), born in 1583.

Oswald married Anne, daughter and co-heir of Ralph Lowe of Mile End, Cheshire and, like his father, was responsible for a considerable family. He was 47 when he died in 1630, his widow surviving him by 41 years! Of his family Edward (III) was born in 1618 and married Jane Meriel the daughter of Richard Saltonstall of Huntwick, near Halifax, Yorkshire. She had been strictly brought up in the principles of Presbyterianism and was very much concerned in the building of the chapel in Pool Fold, Manchester. This was later known as Cross Street Chapel.

To resume our main story. Sir Edward (II) left a will dated 18th December 1660, in which he described himself as '. . . of Rolleston in the County of Stafford'. He directed that his funeral expenses:

'. . . bee moderate, not exceedinge eight hundred pounds nor less than 400^{li}.'

He willed his properties to his Grandmother Anne (M), to his Aunt Anne (N), to his cousin Nicholas of Ancoats (O), cousin Anthony of London, Cousin Anne of Collyhurst and several non-family bequests with the remainder to his sister Mary (P).

The list of beneficiaries is given because the will, although lodged, as if duly proved, in the Bishop's Registry at Chester, seems never to have been effective. It is at considerable variance to a second will which was made, according to the 'Family Memoirs', within a week of his death, dated 13th October 1665 by which, after the expiration of a term of fifteen years the whole of his property passed to Edward Mosley of Hulme (III). There were complicated directions and provisions which were to be observed by the executors in the case of certain circumstances arising but they were not required and the estates and properties passed to Edward.

He was another eminent barrister like his earlier kinsman Edward of Rolleston, and held office as one of the Commissioners for the administration of Justice in Scotland. He continued in this office during the period of the Commonwealth.

Almost as soon as he took possession of his inheritance, threats of legal proceedings from claimants under both wills were forthcoming. Mary (P) sister of the deceased Edward, who found herself disinherited under the second will claimed through her husband, several creditors of the testator claimed payment of their several outstanding debts and elder brother Nicholas tried to enforce part of the will which related to himself.

Arguments dragged on and finally Edward agreed on terms for the partition of the estates. Breadsall Park (Derbyshire), Hulme Hall, Hough End, Didsbury, Withington, Heaton Norris, Chorlton, Cheadle Mosley (Stockport) remained to Sir Edward. His daughter Anne (Q) was to enjoy the life interest of the Manor of Manchester which then was to go to Oswald Mosley, eldest son of Nicholas Mosley of Ancoats.

Edward was knighted by William III at Whitehall in 1689 and died in 1696 leaving only Anne as his heiress, the three sons, Nicholas, Francis and Edward having pre-deceased him. He was buried at Didsbury and his will[44] provides for practically the whole of his estates to go to his daughter Anne and her husband Sir John Bland, whom she married at Chorlton Chapel in 1685 and their male heirs, or £5,000 for their daughter(s) if there be no male heir with the estates going to nephew Oswald

(R). His widow was to receive £150 per year, being due half-yearly at Michaelmas and Lady Day, and the 'Manor of Hulme' which after her death was to revert to their daughter Anne; four pounds per year to the churchwardens of Didsbury for the use of the poor of Withington and Heaton Norris; three pounds per annum for 21 years to the preacher at Didsbury and £50 to be divided amongst his domestic servants. His wife was nominated as his sole executrix and John Frankland, William Garnett and Nathaniel Corles were witnesses.

Sir John Bland (I) of Kippax in Yorkshire was, to say the least of it, an unfortunate choice of husband for Anne. Whatever hopes of a happy and successful marriage there might have been in the beginning, it proved to be a disaster. The 'Family Memoirs' describe him as:

'A youth of good connections, pleasing deportment and great apparent devotion, became his (i.e. Sir Edward's) daughter's declared admirer; her unsuspecting heart was soon captivated by his addresses, and the willing consent of her affectionate parents was as quickly obtained to their union. Sir John was an infant when he succeeded to the baronetcy by the death of an elder brother, and he had not attained the age of twenty-one at the time of his marriage with Miss Mosley on the 31st March 1685. Young however as he was, he had learnt, and could practice with a master's skill the art of duplicity; for when the wealthy heiress had been once obtained, he laid aside his apparent devotion, and rushed into all the dissipation of the fashionable world, regardless of the pain he was thus inflicting upon his fondly-attached wife and her parents. . . .'

Strong words to be used of one's family. Sir John served as Member of Parliament for the Borough of Appleby and later for Pontefract. In spite of the fact that his addiction to gambling and his love of dissipation had squandered most of his wife's considerable fortune and brought them to the verge of ruin, a monument was erected after death and burial at Didsbury which gives anything but an accurate picture of his real character. He died in 1715 (25th October) and Lady Anne lived until 1734.

During her widowhood she lived mostly at Hulme Hall and took a great interest in church affairs in Manchester. Her mother's influence was responsible for her Low Church sympathies and as well as her interest in the Pool Fold Chapel, she was actively concerned with the building of St. Ann's Church to counter the influence of the 'High Church Party' of the Collegiate Church. The new church was so named in compliment to the Queen and Lady Anne and she laid the foundation-stone on the 18th May 1709. She gave generously to the cost of its erection and at its consecration on 12th July 1712 gave some of the communion plate and a velvet covering for the altar.

Lady Anne was the acknowledged leader of Low Church fashion and was for ever trying to outshine Lady Drake of the High Church congregation. She had 'public days' when she rode round in her coach and pair to show off. When she died her will was reasonably straightforward. Most of what was left from her late husband's extravagances went to their son who had the same name as his father; their daughter Meriel Jacob was given £100 and her (Anne's) best diamond ear-rings. In the event of Sir John Bland (II), their son, having no issue the estate was to go to the heirs of Meriel Jacob and failing that to her cousin Francis of Rolleston (S).

Sir John the younger had not only the same name as his dissolute father but had the same characteristic vices. In 1715, the year of the insurrection of the Old Pretender, he was indicted for treason but details of the charge are not known. Very soon his extravagances voided any hope that his mother might have had of the estates staying in the family:

'Their only surviving son, who bore the same name as his father . . . was returned in several Parliaments for the county palatine of Lancaster . . . lived long enough to complete the mischief which his father commenced; the same destructive habit of gambling reduced his splendid patrimoney, and he sold without remorse the whole of the estates which his mother had brought into his family within a few years after her decease.'

Sir John (II) died in 1742 in Bath. He left two sons, Sir John (III) and Sir Hunderford. Both died without issue, Sir John 3rd September 1755 and his brother in 1756. With the latter's passing the line became extinct and the family connection with Chorlton and Hough End ceased.

Towards the end the financial plight became catastrophic.

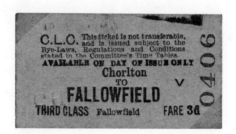

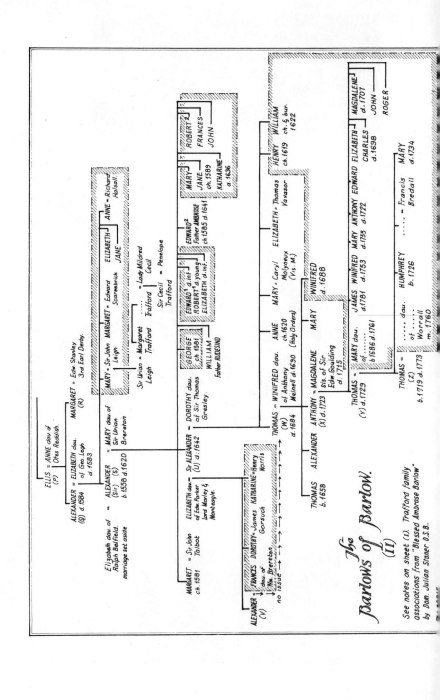

The Barlows of Barlow.
(II)

See notes on sheet (1). Trafford family associations from "Blessed Ambrose Barlow" by Dom. Julian Stoner O.S.B.

Ivor Million records (History of Didsbury) that on 30th June 1752 Sir John (III) mortgaged the Manor of Withington and much land to William Fenwick of Bywell, Northumberland, for £5,000, land in Didsbury to Joshua Cox of Holborn for £8,000 and the Manor of Cheadle Hulme to Richard Shelley of Hanover Square, London, for £3,000. A total of £16,000! A year later, almost to the day (28th June) William Fenwick loaned a further £2,000 and, yet again, another £2,000 on 20th December of the same year.

The estates were sold. Hulme (including a considerable area of land in the township of Chorlton) went to George Lloyd, stated to be of Manchester, but with strong Yorkshire associations and probably of a family with long ties with the Mosleys. The remainder, including Hough End but excluding the lands of the Barlows and the few small owners went to Samuel Egerton of Tatton. In 1758 Samuel Egerton purchased a considerable amount of land, presumably through executors. The oak staircase from Hough End is said to have been taken to Tatton Hall and the old home of Sir Nicholas became a farmhouse, latterly known as Peacock Farm from the birds of that specie which strutted about the yard.

THE BARLOW FAMILY (II)

The Barlows had always been staunch Catholics. With the Reformation their adherence to the Old Faith remained unshaken and much of the recorded story of the family is concerned with religious matters.

Ellis Barlow and his wife had one son and one daughter. The daughter was Margaret (R) the wife of Edward Stanley, third Earl Derby. The son was Alexander (Q) who married Elizabeth, daughter of George Leigh of Manchester. He was Member of Parliament for Wigan 1547–1557[45] and was the first member of the family to suffer persecution for his faith. In general it would seem, that there had been little persecution of the Catholics in Lancashire but it increased as the Protestant influence of the developing industrial areas was encouraged by Elizabeth I's penal enactments.

In 1584 Barlow Hall was extensively rebuilt and in this same year some fifty Roman Catholic gentlemen in Lancashire had their houses searched in pretence of looking for hidden priests.

As priests appeared to move freely from house to house it would seem that this was a token exercise. In the surviving account it is mentioned that Mr. Barlow was so ill as not to be able to sit on his horse. This did not save him and he was taken to Manchester where a measure of sympathy was shown for he was placed in the charge of a local gentleman (whose name is not recorded) and in whose house he died in August 1584. He was buried in Didsbury Chapel on 26th August. His gaoler, we are told, was so impressed by his dignity and forbearance in the face of adversity that he himself embraced the same faith.

Alexander's son, Sir Alexander (S) was married twice, the first being an infant marriage, as was common at the time, to Elizabeth daughter and co-heiress of Ralph Belfield of Clegg, Lancashire. He was aged four when this marriage took place. In 1574, when 16 years of age, having refused to ratify the arrangement, he sued for, and was granted, a divorce on 21st October. In his testimony on oath he is reputed to have said that he never:

> '. . . did at any tyme ratifie the said pretensed marriage solempnized (*sic*) between them, for he doth not remember that ev he was maried to the said Elizabeth or spake the words of matrimony to her, he was so young the same tyme it is said he was maried to the said Elizabeth.'

Free of this arrangement, he married Mary, daughter of Sir Urian Brereton of Honford (i.e. Handforth), Cheshire, by whom, to use the common phrase of the time, 'he had issue a numerous family'. The family tree in Booker shows nine children four sons and five daughters but in a footnote (p. 265) reference is made to a copper engraved plate of Sir Alexander which gives additionally, William, John 'who died . . . in Spayne', Edward died an infant, Robert died young and Elizabeth died an infant.

He was knighted, with his son Alexander (U) at Whitehall on the occasion of the coronation of James I in 1603. In his will of 1617 he affirmed his belief:

> '. . . to be a saved soñte and a member and coeheire of that celestiall Kingdome, and that I die a true and p'fecte recusante catholicke. . . .'

and directed:

> '. . . that yf yt fortune I die wᵗʰin twentye myles of my house at Barlowe that my sayd bodye be leyde in Dids-

burye Churche as neere unto my father as may be, and
that there be noe pompe nor solemintye used or donne
for me. . . .'

There was not a great deal to distribute, but:

'. . . my will and mynde ys that xx^s be geaven and distributed amonge the poore of Hardaye, Chowlerton and
Marslache by xij^d a peace dowle (i.e. dole) to praye for
my soule, and the same distribution to be at the discre-
tione of my executors wthin one yeare nexte after mt
deathe.'

His wish to be buried at Didsbury was set aside by his
executors and he was laid to rest at the Collegiate Church on
21st April 1620. In a letter from one Leonard Smedley to
Sir Richard St. George[46] the funeral is referred to:

'Sir Alexander Barlow of Barlow ob. circa April 27,
1620, and was buried at Manchester Church by torch light,
whose exōrs cannot yet resolve whether to have a funeral
or noe by reson sume of them ar yet in the south p'ts
neere London &c. but within 20 daies I am to receave
an absolute answer.'

Of his children, Edward (T) became the most distinguished
of the whole family of Barlow.

The feudal lords of South Lancashire were almost entirely
Catholic and the power of their undisputed leaders, the Stanleys,
Earls of Derby, was almost absolute. The Barlows, as we have
already noted, had a marriage connection with the Stanleys
through Margaret (daughter of Ellis Barlow) marrying Edward
the third Earl, but there was an even stronger tie by virtue of the
wife of Sir Alexander (S) being Mary, the daughter of Sir Urian
Brereton of Handforth and of Sir John Stanley's widow, who
had married Sir Urian on the death of Sir John.[47]

But in spite of these strong associations with Catholicism,
there were times when faith wavered. William Barlow remains
one of the mysteries for what is recorded of his origins does not
agree with known facts. It is not impossible that William,
having failed to return to the fold after a period of deviation,
was so effectively renounced by the family that no hint of the
truth remains in the family records.

One story asserts that he was a child of a second marriage
of Alexander Barlow (Q) to Mary, daughter of Sir Urian

Brereton, an assertion which cannot be upheld on the count that Elizabeth pre-deceased Alexander by only eight months so that a second marriage would hardly be possible let alone that there should be 'a numerous family'. Additionally the certified pedigree shows Mary to have been the wife of Alexander the younger (S). In the Stanley Papers[48] William is described as the son of Alexander (S) but here their dates of birth conflict. Alexander was born in 1558 and William (according to his biographers) about the same time.

William was certainly a member of the family and with that we must rest satisfied. Dr. Cosin, Dean of the Arches, was responsible for his upbringing and entered ihm as a student of Trinity College, Cambridge in 1580. By 1584, in which year he graduated in Arts, he had transferred to St. John's; 1587 saw him gain his M.A., in 1590 elected a fellow of Trinity Hall and 1597 a Doctorate of Divinity. He was given the living of Orpington, Kent, was chaplain to the archbishop and soon afterwards became chaplain to the Queen. He became rector of St. Dunstan's in the East and Prebendary of St. Pauls. His preferment was rapid for in 1601 he was installed Prebendary of Westminster and in 1603 Dean of Chester. Archbishop Whitgift selected him to produce the account of the Episcopacy Conference held at Hampton Court in the presence of James I in 1603. 1605 saw him installed as Prebendary of Canterbury and in the same year Bishop of Rochester. Here he remained for three years and was translated to the Bishopric of Lincoln in 1608. He died in 1613, numbering amongst his other accomplishments that of being one of the translators of the Bible.

Being successful in the Church seems to have paid off for if there was little for Sir Alexander (S) to disburse, Bishop William could well afford his generosity.[49]

Even Edward, son of Sir Alexander (S) seems to have deviated from his faith for a short time in his youth.The dowager Lady Davenport seems to have been the influence which brought him back, with a 'friend's father'. Edward as a youth is said to have served as a 'page'[50] in the household of his maternal cousin Sir Urian Legh[51] where, there is little doubt, he came under the strong Protestant influence of the Traffords.[52] It was probably in 1607 (he would then be about 22) that he reverted to the faith of his fathers and started to study for the priesthood. He studied under the Jesuits in Anchin College, matriculating on 23rd February 1608. An older brother had graduated through the English College and University of Douai some six years earlier. He had taken the name of Father Rudeshind and Dom Stoner identifies him as William though Booker's much earlier reference states that his baptismal name is not known.

Edward had gone to Douai on matriculating and in 1610 was sent to Spain to study philosophy. It is possible that during his stay in Spain the two brothers met but if not they no doubt did so in the following years when they were both at Douai, Edward at the University and William at the recently-opened English monastery there.

Edward returned to England in 1613 and under the penal laws then in force was imprisoned for several months in London. William's choice of vocation had, however, inspired Edward and he returned to Douai to become a monk, adopting the name of Ambrose. Of the eighteen brethren in the little monastry, seven were from Lancashire.

For three years Father Ambrose dedicated himself to a novitiate of prayer. He led an austere life and was entirely satisfied with, and derived great pleasure from, his devotion.

South-east Lancashire was the home of relatively few Catholic families, so much so that when, in 1639, a list of Catholic parishes and priests in Lancashire was drawn up for the purpose of a collection, the Hundred of Salford was excluded. South-west Lancashire was quite a different matter for there the nature of the terrain was such that local conditions had remained almost unchanged and the population almost wholly Catholic. It was here that Father Ambrose's life-work lay.

He travelled around a circuit which, we are told, occupied a week out of each month. He lived, when not on circuit, at Morley's Hall near Leigh and travelled everywhere on foot. In his 56th year he suffered a stroke which deprived him of the use of one side[53] and made it necessary for him to both use a horse and employ a servant.

He was a man mild in manner, witty in conversation and cheerful even in adversity. In his youth, at least, he would hold tenaciously to what he thought was his right, as in the case of Alice Smalley's will.[54] His clothes were simple, of grey-frise, a long-waisted jerkin and doublet, his breeches tied above his knees. His hat was described as 'The best hat that ever I saw him wear I would not have given two groats for. . . .' He wore a threadbare band around his neck and on his feet a pair of 'scurvy old slip-shoes'. His poor clothing was matched by his frugal living, his usual diet consisting of curds, buttermilk, white meat and very little to drink.

Three times in the year, Christmas, Easter and Whitsun, he entertained all and sundry. The menu was usually boiled beef and pottage, mince pies, goose and groats. Usually the more honourable members of the gathering waited on the poorer and afterwards dined off their leavings. On leaving they were given a groat in alms and to those whose need was great a coat.

In his years of ministration he seems to have been a friend to all. For some reason he steadfastly refused to leave Lancashire. On one occasion when asked to visit a Cheshire house he refused with the explanation that priests did much good in Lancaster Castle but in Chester gaol he never heard of any good that they did!

Father Ambrose had a premonition and was resigned to his ultimate incarceration in Lancaster Castle, but he continued his work openly. He seems to have suffered short periods of imprisonment from time to time but the curtain rose on the last act on 7th March 1641, when Charles I bowed to his Parliament and issued a decree by which all Jesuits and seminary priests were required to leave the country within one month. Father Ambrose did not come into either category (he was a Benedictine) and was too weak to make a journey, but the opponents of that for which he stood did not inquire into the technicalities. On Easter morning, six weeks after the decree ·of Charles, the sequence of events which culminated in his death commenced.

The Vicar of Leigh, the Rev. John Gantley, proposed to his congregation that they should '. . . do a service to God' by arresting 'that noted popish priest'. He suggested that they should undertake the duty at once rather than wait until after mattins for then they would apprehend Father Ambrose in the midst of his flock.

So the congregation, some four hundred we are told, with

clubs and swords and any other weapons they could find, streamed off, the vicar leading with his surplice billowing behind him, towards Morley's Hall. Father Ambrose had finished Mass and was preaching to a flock of a hundred or so on the subject of patience when the mob appeared. He would not be persuaded to hide nor allow his followers to offer any resistance. So weak that he could only sit on his horse with someone behind him for support, he was taken to Lancaster with an escort of sixty men.[55]

His health appears to have improved somewhat by the time he appeared at the summer assizes. Attempts by his friends to ease his lot were rebuked and he made it clearly understood that he regarded death for his belief as the most desirable end. He read the book of Boetius 'De Consolatione' until a warder took it from him, whereupon he is reputed to have said with a smile 'If you take this little book away I will betake myself to that great book from which Boetius learned his wholesome doctrine, and that book you can never take away from me.' Thereafter he spent much of his time in mental prayer.

His trial commenced on 7th September before Sir Robert Heath. Father Ambrose confessed openly to being a priest and to have practiced that office for upwards of twenty years. In the interrogation he yielded nothing and even rebuked his judge: 'I know and acknowledge you judge, but in such causes only as belong to the temporal court and tribunal; but in spiritual matters, and in things belonging to the court of conscience, be pleased to take notice that I am judge, and therefore I tell you plainly, that if by that unjust law you sentence me to die, it will be to my salvation and your damnation.'

He was found guilty and pronounced so in the usual form. His reply was a cheerful 'Thanks be to God.' and a prayer to the Almighty to have mercy on all who had been concerned with his death.

On 3rd September, a week before his death, his brother, Father Rudeshind resigned as honorary Cathedral Prior of Coventry, which the General Chapter then bestowed on Father Ambrose. He never learned of the honour.

Friday, 10th September 1641, was the day of his execution. Carrying a small cross of wood which he had fashioned himself, he was laid upon the hurdle and taken to the place of execution. Arrived there he walked three times round the gallows, the cross clasped to his breast and repeating the Miserere, and those ministers who in their zeal would have argued with him about religion, he rebuked by telling them that he had other things to do at that moment than listen to their fooleries.

He was hanged by the neck until almost dead, cut down and disembowelled whilst still in this wretched condition, beheaded and quartered. His skull was set on a spike over the gateway as an object lesson to others and in a short time it was pecked clean by crows and other carnivorous birds.

Francis Downes of Wardley rescued the skull and took it to Wardley Hall. It must have taken a great deal of courage to ask for such a controversial relic. The Downes were relatives of the Barlows[53] being referred to as 'cousins' but the relationship was very much more tenuous. The skull remains at Wardley, in a niche on the side of the staircase. As the house is now the official home of the Catholic Bishop of Salford, it is not possible to view it.[56]

The church on nearby Princess Parkway was dedicated to St. Ambrose but though in respect of Father Ambrose, the dedication was actually to St. Ambrose of Milan. However, on the occasion of the canonization of Father Ambrose, the Papal Authorities consented to a joint dedication to St. Ambrose of Milan and St. Ambrose Barlow. The hall bell from Barlow Hall was given by Chorlton Golf Club to the Diocese of Salford who passed it into the care of the church where now it plays its part in the celebration of the Mass.

With the death of Father Ambrose the fire went from the family. It was like a roman-candle with the Martyr as the last glorious burst of fire. There followed a short dull fizzle and an inglorious end.

Edward's eldest brother Alexander (U) married twice. In the first case to Elizabeth, daughter of Edward Parker, Lord Morley and Monteagle, and secondly to Dorothy, daughter of Sir Thomas Gresley. Alexander died in 1642 and the new lord of Barlow was another Alexander (V), the fourth in succession. He was the only surviving son of his father's first marriage and was married to Frances, daughter of William Brereton of Ashley.

He died without issue in (or about) 1654 and the estates passed to Thomas (W), his half-brother and eldest son of Sir Alexander's second marriage.

Thomas left little on record. He married Winifred, the daughter of Anthony Meinell and died in 1684. His successor was Anthony (X) whose elder brothers Thomas and Alexander pre-deceased him.

Anthony's name appears in the List of Papists who were required by an Act of the first year of the reign of George I to register their estates. He returned the value as £171 9s. His wife was Magdalene, sister of Sir Edward Goulding and he died in 1723. His will (dated 3rd August 1722) is complex but indicates a split in family unity:

> 'But in case there shall then be any interruption in the descent to my immediate heir occasioned by the corruption blood of the said Thomas Barlow or Anthony Barlow now attainted on high treason, upon trust then to convey the same to such person or persons as his or their heirs who should then have been my immediate heir-at-law in case the blood of the said Thomas Barlow and Anthony Barlow had never been corrupted as aforesaid.'

possibly revealing a sympathy with the Stuart cause.[57]

Thomas (Y), in spite of the reference in the will, appears to have inherited. His marriage was not successful and the quarrels between him and his wife, involving members of the family, finally resulted in his undergoing a term of imprisonment in Lancaster Castle, awarded as a penalty for attempting the murder of his wife. He died of gaol fever, in prison, in 1729, and the inventory of his goods and chattels compiled by his widow (whose maiden name has escaped recording) was claimed to be false by his sister Winifred. The action against the widow is quoted by Booker[58] and the impression is gained that Thomas was anything but well off. Perhaps the two more interesting points are the evidence of William Fendown, aged 19, that Mary Barlow, his mistress, had told him that her husband had once fired two pistols 'at the same time' at her, and that once she allowed him to feel the scar which had been left on the back of her head, and the list of charges which Mary Barlow claimed she had paid on account of the deceased:

Paid on account of yᵉ decd yᵉ followᵍ items:

Pd. Mr. Postlethwaite of Lancaster by yᵉ hands of Mr. Broom, being a Book Debt owing by Mr. Barlow for money lent him	7	3	0
Pd. him for necessaries and attendance on Mr. B. in his sickness	1	17	7
Pd. for yᵉ use of yᵉ Bed he lay on to the Gaoler of Lancaster		7	6
Pd. for a Shroud and making	1	3	3
Pd. for 18 paid of gloves and yᵉ Pall at his funeral	1	19	8
Pd. for a Coffin		16	0
Pd. for yᵉ Church Dues and attendance at yᵉ funeral and expenses	1	15	8
Pd. Dr. Bracken's Bill for Physic	2	10	3
Pd. the Coroner's fee for his Inquest on yᵉ Dead		13	4

The court found that the inventory was not a true one.

And so we come to the last lord of Barlow. Another Thomas (Z). He married a Miss Worrall in 1760 and died in 1773 without leaving a son for the properties to pass to. His will required that all his personal effects, furniture, plate, etc., be converted into cash as quickly as possible and added to his real estate. His widow's annuity was to be provided for from the rents of the estate to be held in trust by Samuel Egerton of Tatton, William Tatton of Wythenshawe, John Houghton of Baguley and Michael Walton of Manchester. There were gifts to relatives and provision for dealing with almost any contingency. If need be everything was to be sold by the executors and the money divided between the surviving relatives. William Tatton, John Houghton and Michael Walton, probably appreciating the possible complications and the consequent personal inconveniences, renounced their executorship. Two years after the proving of the will, 2nd August 1785, the estate was auctioned by the authority of an Act of Parliament obtained to facilitate the sale. The Egertons of Tatton were the purchasers. So passed the Barlows.

CHORLTON IN THE XVI CENTURY

There can be little doubt that Chorlton's development was subject to the same influences as other similar communities, and that its inhabitants behaved like people elsewhere. The manner of arable farming and the process of encroachment on to common land in particular, applied to such evidence and knowledge available for our use, makes it possible to evolve a picture of Chorlton in the Middle Ages which is very probably correct.

The pieces of the jig-saw are all straightforward. To take them in order:

i. The field unit was the 'acre' which was ploughed in strips or rows of length dictated by the ability of a pair of oxen to pull the primitive ploughs without faltering. This length, irrespective of the difference in size of the Lancashire acre as compared with the Statute acre, was fairly consistent at about 220 yards (from which is derived 'furlong' or 'furrow-long').

ii. Between each group of rows and at the ends were 'balks' which were uncultivated, being used for turning ploughs, as a dump for stones and as the normal paths from strip to strip and place to place.

iii. Every community had its measure of common land, usually in the centre of the village, used for common grazing and recreation. From time to time encroachment on to this land was made—often by the Lord of the Manor (in which case the villagers would have been unwise to object) but sometimes by one of their own number, or strangers, when no objection might be made because it was not considered important or because the villagers did not appreciate their rights.

Let us now take the facts as we have them. The name 'acre' is perpetuated in Acres Road and Acres Passage, both of which run from Beech Road to High Lane. Before the building up of this area the fields were all known as Row Acres. The mean length of Whitelow, Stockton, Acres, Chequers (late Church) and Wilton Roads is tolerably close to one furlong. It is not possible to be exact between the row acres because the balks had no particular width, but a simple pacing and measurement of the map reveals a significant relationship to twenty-two yards, the old rod, pole or perch which, like the furlong, stemmed from strip farming. The Tithe Map of 1845 shows fields of similar proportions north of Edge Lane and Sandy Lane; of these we must have some reservation.

If we study a large scale map of the area round the Green, it is obvious that the building which is now the Horse & Jockey

Inn must have been built after Beech Road became a thorough-
fare for the rear boundary of the property is in alignment with
the north side of Beech Road. The reputed date of the building
is 'about 1500'.

Let us now look at the brook side. On the flat area between
the brook and the bowling green (now built on) was the village
fish pond. It is marked as such on the 1845 map and described in
the schedule as 'Fish Pond & Waste', owned by Wilbraham
Egerton and tenanted by George Whitelegg. This was a well-
chosen spot for a constant supply of fresh water would flow
through quite naturally and the fish could be easily kept captive
by a simple form of weir. No doubt fish caught in the Mersey
were kept here until required. Reference has been made to the
bowling green. Bowls in one form or another is a very ancient
game and is widespread throughout western Europe. Its popularity probably stemmed from the fact that the equipment
required is simple and in its less sophisticated form can be
readily made. Certainly there were several bowling greens in
Chorlton in the early XIX century. It is probable that tucked
away in a corner of the common land, the inhabitants had a
bowling place where they congregated to pass away the summer
evenings. No more suitable spot could be found than the present
site of the green behind the Bowling Green Hotel, and, of course,
a drink or two would be a natural complement to a game.
Somebody would satisfy the demand and though the licence of
the Bowling Green Hotel is reputed to date only from 1693,
this does not rule out the possibility that there was a retailer at
an earlier date.

Now we must look at the site of the Church. The first chapel
was probably provided by the Barlows but however much the
villagers valued the gift, nobody would wish to give up such a
large area of his land and so, as was done elsewhere, the church
would be built on common land. This was sensible, it was for
the community, it should be built on the community's land.
Hence the building was sited on the shoulder above the area
liable to flooding and conveniently placed for the people of
Hardy on the other side of the brook. The common land is
now getting rather smaller.

On the east side of the area there was, apparently, more
encroachment for we are informed that the National Schools

were built on the site of a cottage, but on the west side where the boundary remained reasonably undisturbed there seems to have been but one minor instance by which the barn (or its predecessor) now restricts the exit from the Green to Brookburn Road. The date of the licensing of the churchyard for burials is not known, the earliest gravestone recorded is 1725. The curious shape of the yard suggests that the barn was built before the graveyard was defined, in which case the first burials may not have been much before the start of the XVIII century.

Thus the Green may have assumed its shape. Later the first National Schools were rebuilt, 1845, and the odd space eventually filled in by Zetland Terrace, 1883. Ivy Green Farm, adjacent to the church (or 'Greenwood's Farm') reached out towards the Pinfold which had long been established by the side of the graveyard. At some time early in the XIX century the triangular centre which developed out of the paths across the area was hedged by Samuel Wilton and so became the most blatant piece of encroachment of them all. In 1895 it reverted to the public, having been latterly in the occupation of Miss Wilton (who lived in one of the cottages now embraced in the Horse & Jockey) as a garden and orchard.

On the sketch maps the story of the conjectured centre of the township is told much more clearly than by words—but it must be remembered that whilst it is probably accurate, it is still the result of conjecture.

THE CHURCH AND THE VILLAGE

In the Domesday Inquest the parish of Manchester was dismissed in a single sentence within the entry relating to the Royal Manor of Salford:

> 'The church of St. Mary and the church of St. Michael held in Manchester one carucate of land quit from every due save (Dane) geld.'

This referred to a church dedicated to St. Mary situated, in all probability where the Cathedral now stands, and the church at Ashton-under-Lyne, probably a daughter church. The population of the whole area was sparse, particularly by today's standards.

The founding of additional chapels was often associated with local families who made their private chapels available to their tenants or built chapels for their tenant's use. The Long-fords, as lords of the manor of Withington established the first chapel in the parish of Manchester after Domesday at Didsbury in 1235.[59] Stretford Chapel was established by 1413 as a chapel of the Trafford family though there is evidence that an oratory existed by 1326.[60]

In 1512, or thereabouts, Chorlton Chapel was established, probably by the Barlow family, and for the first few years of its existence it would see the celebration of the Mass. A drawing of this first building exists[61] though no authority for it is known. It is shown to have been a building typical of the domestic archi-tecture of the district, half timbered and very simple. It was rec-tangular in ground plan with a small extension on the east end which would form the chancel. Stone provided the foundation wall, to an estimated height of about eighteen inches, and a wood framing, very regular in its arrangement, rested on this. One assumes the obvious that the framing was filled with lath and plaster—especially as clay was to be found in ample quantities so near at hand. This form of construction was common in dwelling houses in the neighbourhood. The roof was steeply pitched and provided ample protection for the walls by a generous overhanging of the eaves.

The gable ends were protected by plain bargeboards, and surmounted by a graceful finial. A small belfry and wind vane surmounted the western end and a sundial was positioned over the arched south door which would seem to have been the main entrance. A small vestry door is shown adjacent to the chancel. For its period the building seems to have been well endowed with windows, the south wall (and, one imagines, the north wall, too), had two four light square-headed windows, a similar three light window illuminated the end wall of the chancel with two similar small windows to give side lighting.

The surroundings are sylvan, but one must allow for some artistic licence. It may be reasonably assumed that since the old church was closed and the new one opened the following year, the replacement was built on the same site. If this is so, the graveyard shown is too generous on the south side.

The chapel was at first in the diocese of Lichfield, and for its first few years would adhere to the Old Faith. In 1540, as a part of the parish of Manchester, it was transferred to Chester.

In 1553 it was referred to in a commission from the Duchy of Lancaster, in Queen Mary's name, as being one of those places which had not handed in its bells, challice, plate, etc., and money as had been required by an enactment of 7 Edward VI. One could hardly call the chapel rich even by the standard of those days for the commission valued the goods and chattels at the princely sum of 2s 8d! In 1573 the Archbishop of York directed an injunction to the Master or Warden of the Collegiate Church concerning the 'diligent and constant preaching every Sunday in the church of Manchester or in one of the chapels' which direction included Chorlton, as did a prohibition, some six years later, of pipers and minstrels, the promotion of baiting on the Sabbath (most likely bear baiting would be intended), the ringing of church bells, the holding of wakes and feasts, gaming and the observance of superstitions.

It would seem that from the beginning certain lands were attached to the church, the income received from 'farming out' these tithes being paid to the Parish Church at Manchester so that the chapel was left very much to fend for itself. What these lands were in Chorlton in the early years is not known, but in 1566 Alexander Barlow (Q) farmed the tithes of Chorlton Chapel and was plaintiff in a case of mismanagement of church estates brought against Thomas Herle, the Warden of Manchester.

As a district chapel Chorlton, in common with those of Didsbury, Birch and Denton in the Manor of Withington, and its near neighbour, Stretford, had no rigid bounds but difficulties of travel would normally restrict each to its own locality. Even so, the registers suggest that there was some fringe movement which might have been due to there being no minister available at Chorlton at a particular time. The entry in the Didsbury Register of baptisms for 1591–92:

> 'Marche 2, Henrye ye sonne of Robt. Hulme de Chorleton by Ellin Barlow de Stretford'

suggests that sometimes it was convenient to go out of the 'parish'.

In 1598 (13th September) the Visitation Returns refer to the chapel in these terms:

> 'Chowlerton Chapel, no curate but a reader who keepeth a school.'

and in 1604 the Visitation recorded that the

> 'Lector or Reader at Chorleton Chapel'

one Roger Worthington was reported to the Bishop for letting
out money on usury. He confessed that:

>'. . . that he lent out iiij^{li} after ij^s in ye pound and not
>above. . . .'

Where he got his money to lend out is not known but he was
instructed to pay:

>'. . . into ye poor mans box at Cholreton ij^s and to refraine
>hereafter.'

Occasionally we get a glimpse of the affairs of the community as, for instance, when in 1598 Nicholas Langeford
asserted his sole right to dig for marle cloddes and turves on
Chorlton More, against William Barlowe, James Brownehill,
Laurence Baguley, Edmund Hunt and Richard Chorlton, or
in 1599 when John Trafford deposed that half the yearly tithe
corn of Chorlton had been worth £6 13s 4d during the last
six years. A levy was agreed in 1582 to provide 40 great oxen
at 53s. 4d. a piece for the Royal Table; it was assessed in 1631
that of every £100 contributed by the Lancashire Hundreds
towards this 'Taxation for Ox Money', Withington's share (of
which Chorlton was presumably considered a part) was
£1 12s. 9d. and Stretford's 8s. 0d.

In 1612 Sir Nicholas Mosley left £100, to be paid in annual
instalments of £5 to a schoolmaster who should teach at the
chapel and read prayers there thrice a week. Who this schoolmaster was, probably considering himself 'passing rich' on £5
a year, is not recorded, but John Dickenson who was licensed as
reader and schoolmaster in 1617 would enjoy some benefit from
Sir Nicholas's benefaction. The endowment was too scanty (if,
indeed, any existed) to attract a properly qualified resident curate
but in 1636 the Rev. John Bradshaw held the office. In this year
the little chapel saw what was probably its most spectacular
wedding when Sir Edward Mosley (I) married the daughter of
Sir Gervais Cutler of Stainboro', Yorkshire. Bradshaw, it can
be assumed, suitably impressed Sir Edward for in 1639 he was
appointed to the more desirable office at Didsbury. His post at
Chorlton passed to the Rev. John Pollett.

The earliest parish registers are now lost but Crofton (HS.I.
212) refers to a stray transcript of the registers at Chester
recording that in 1639 there were ten baptisms and the 'Chappell
Wardens' were John Williamson and Edmund Coppocke.[62]

John Pollett was curate when the Law established the Presbyterian form of church government, but he did not agree with the new order, refusing to amend his teaching to conform. It might have been thought that such reactionary behaviour would have suited the mood of his flock, but they teazed and harassed him and finally, being charged with maintaining episcopacy and defending the use of the surplice and Book of Common Prayer, he was dispossessed in 1647.

But even greater troubles were to come. The Rev. Richard Benson was his immediate successor and he very soon found himself in acute disagreement with the elders of the congregation. The 6th January 1647–48 saw them summoned before the classis on a charge of using 'railing words'. Booker reports on the depositions taken[63] and it would seem that the trouble stemmed from cross words between Benson and the elders. In spite of the disagreement he held the curacy until his death in 1651 and was described by the Parliamentary Commission of 1650 as 'a painfull godly preaching minister' which can be construed as one wishes!

In 1641 Parliament decreed that those over 18 years should subscribe to a 'Protestation' that they followed the Protestant form of worship. Fortunately the return for Chorlton has survived. From it we learn that there were in Chorlton 55, in Martledge 13, and in Hardy 16 signatories, making a total of 84. There is no note of those not signing so it would seem that it was not considered necessary to extend it to Barlow and the family there.

It is not known why Hough End was transferred from the township of Chorlton to that of Withington, but as it happened about this time it may have been solely the result of it being found more convenient to organize the protestation of those living there from Withington rather than Chorlton.

1644 found Chorlton in a Civil War of which it probably knew little and cared less, but it was reminded of it on 20th May in that year when Prince Rupert camped on 'Barloe More' en route to aid Bolton and Lathom House. The evidence points to Barlow Moor and Didsbury Moor being the same and lying between Princess Road and Palatine Road, Didsbury, but the impact on the district would be considerable. There promised to be an even greater impact the following year when William

Brereton, the Parliamentary leader, decided that the Royalist forces would enter Lancashire by way of Stockport or Stretford and the strategic position for his troops would be in the mid position, Barlow Moor. He gave his orders to Col. Ashton at Chester:

'It is this day ordered that Coll: Ashton wth his Rgt of ffoote now in Cheshire march into Lancash: and that ye sd Coll Ashton doe bring ye sd Regt as Compleate as possible to ye Randezvous at Barlymore in Lancash: upon Thursday and there Remaine in a body until further Order according to ye Command received from ye Committee of both kingdomes and ye Lord Farefax.

Wm Brereton.'

But a local battle was not to be joined. Charles marched off in the direction of Leicester, Naseby and disaster. Some troops, according to Brereton writing to Col. Fairfax, assembled:

'. . . there are already drawne to ye Rendezvous at Barlow More the Cheshire horse, Colonell Duckenfields and part of Colonel Ashtons Regiments of foote but ye Lancashire Horse and Colonell Holland's Regimt are not yet marched thither from ye service against Latham.

. . . The number hereof that may depended upon wee believe will not amount to much above 1000 foote and fower of five (i.e. four or five . . .) hundred horse and Dragoons wch are only ye Cheshire horse.'

Meanwhile there was still trouble at the chapel. 1644 saw James Parkinson elected as 'ruling-elder'—an offlce which trespassed on the duties which had hitherto been largely the responsibility of the minister. In 1646 Nathaniel Taylor accused Parkinson, and produced proof to the First Lancashire Classis on 16th March 1646–7, of a wide range of offences which, it was suggested, made him unsuited to this office. The evidence and counter-evidence produced makes bewildering reading; Parkinson was accused of '. . . fornication; to ground w^ch

is produced ye register of Ashton-under-line, Mr. Stirrups hand, of a daughter genita ante nuptias, also a sonne borne within twenty seven weeks after marriage. Thus far ye register.'

He was accused of slander and swearing,

'. . . Thomas Blomiley saith he heard him swear and curse above two years.'
To all these was added an accusation of violence:
'. . . James Charlton saith he cast a pot and a fflagon at the face of another man (within a year) and Thomas Blomiley saith he struck his daughter.'
In mitigation it was stated that in the former case,
'. . . Thomas (James?) Parkinson being first called a knave.'

Reading further into the evidence recorded by Booker in full gives the impression that it was the outcome of a village feud, and how the village must have loved the spicy tittle tattle which would be associated with:

'James Chorlton and John Barlow, elders of Chorlton, next deputed by the classis to examine Ellen Hurbboate (not able to come to ye classis) concerning a second born to the s^d Parkinson upon ye s^d New Yeares Day; that it was borne without haire or nayles; that shee considered it was borne before time' and from Jane Jones, '. . . saith that she saw ye s^d child within a day y^t it was borne, and y^t it was very weak, could not suck of about eight weeks, and she believeth y^t it was borne about eight weeks before time.'

But this evidence that the child was born in wedlock was attacked by the accusers who produced Ralph Barlow of Ashton on Mersey Bank who affirmed:

'. . . Joane Warburton, afterwards Joane Jones, was a light woman of her love both before marriage, in that state, and in her widow-hood; that some discourse passing (during the time of her widowhood) betwixt ye said widow Jones and ye said James Parkinson, being desired by ye said Parkinson, this examinant was present, when ye said widow Jones denyed y^t ever she reported of ye said James Parkinson evell behind his back; that ye said Parkinson desired he might have her good report and she should have his.'[64]

The case dragged on for a little more than a year and finally the classis decided that Mr. Parkinson was not a fit and proper person to exercise the duties of ruling-elder.

Before this case had been settled the classis was confronted by an appeal from the eldership of Chollerton to resolve a difference between Nathaniel Taylor (the same) and his brother

Samuel. In February 1648–9, Samuel was cleared and Nathaniel was ordered to acknowledge his error before the classis.[65] Whether he did or not we will never know.

In 1650 the endowment of £69 was jointly held by the Chapel and the schoolmaster, and though it had not been acceptable for Roger Worthington to lend out his own money at interest for his own benefit, it was the accepted principle by which endowments were made to earn money to pay for the curate or schoolmaster. In 1704 a return to the Bishop of Chester gave the annual income as £1 15s, taking pains to point out that £80 of the £100 left by Sir Oswald Mosley in 1612 had been lost by a tradesman in Manchester to whom it had been lent.

Richard Benson died in 1651 and was buried on 27th May at Stretford. His successor was John Adcroft (or Odcroft), who had been curate at Stretford for two years. He stayed until 1654, and his brief ministry seems to have been notable for the embarrassment caused to the classis by his disregard for their authority. In his turn he was followed by James Jackson. Mr. Jackson was unordained when he accepted the office but was ordained the following year (together with Jeremy Scholes) in Chorlton Chapel. Of Mr. Scholes we shall hear more.

A return of 1655 gave forty-two persons in the township rated for the relief of the poor. Mr. Barlow of Barlow Hall was rated at £2 8s. 4d. and John Barlow, James Chorleton, Mr. Mosley of Birch House and Henry Rigbie were included in the list.

By 1658 it would seem that Mr. Jackson was feeling the financial pinch of his office. The classis were as unwilling to accept his resignation (probably fearful that they could not replace him with the miserable stipend available) as the congregation were to forego the very great good that they claimed he had accomplished. As a result the classis appointed a panel of ministers to visit Chorlton and see if the stipend could be increased. That they undertook their task in style is evident for we are told 'Mr. Harrison was desired to preach a sermon on the subject. . . .' (generosity, that is), ' . . . and Mr. Heyrick, Mr. Angier and Mr. Newcome accompanied him.'—the result was seemingly satisfactory to all parties for Mr. Jackson agreed to remain a further year, the congregation agreed to make up the stipend from £35 to £50, it was promised that every effort would be made to raise a further £5 over and above the increase already agreed, and pressure would be exerted for the payment of some outstanding debts. Mr. Jackson did not exercise his agreed option of resigning after twelve months if the agreement was not kept for he was still in office in October 1662.

In 1662 the boundaries of the township were defined with tolerable accuracy—previously the bounds had been but vague. No doubt the increasing national concern over taxation played some part in demanding more accurate definition.

Mr. Jackson had left Chorlton by 1672, his place had been taken by a Mr. Richardson whose christian name is not recorded.[66] In this year the Rev. Jeremy Scholes, it will be remembered he was ordained at the same time as Mr. Jackson, and who had gone from Stretford to Norton, near Dronfield, from whence he had been ejected in 1662, took advantage of the 'Indulgences to Dissenters' of 1672 to obtain a licence to use his own house in Salford as a Presbyterian meeting house, and on 27th July 1672 obtained a similar licence to use the 'out-housings' of Thomas Lowe in Chorlton for the same purpose. He died in 1685 and was buried in Manchester Churchyard.

At this time, 1673, Chorlton Chapel was in the gift of the Dean and Chapter of Manchester who exercised their right of patronage, appointing two wardens, one for Chorlton and one for Hardy. In 1680 Mr. Richardson, Edward perhaps, died.

Chorlton Chapel's second wedding of note took place in 1685 when Lady Ann Mosley married Sir John Bland. A silver chalice was presented to the chapel by Lady Ann; one supposes that the celebration of communion formed a part of the ceremony and the gift would probably be used on that occasion for the first time.

Between the ministry of the Rev. James Jackson or Mr. Richardson's death in 1680, and 1691 when we find reference to the Rev. Joshua Hyde officiating, there is a lack of information. In 1691 Mr. Hyde was nominated by Sir John Egerton to the curacy of Denton and we are unaware of the date when he came here. During his time at Chorlton he may not have been wholly ordained, perhaps being in deacon's orders and combining the office of curate with that of schoolmaster. Again, with the translation of Mr. Hyde a further veil is drawn over the ministrations of the chapel of Chorlton until 1716, except insofar as Warden Wroe is on record as stating in 1707 that:

'Chorleton and Stretford have no settled curates, for want of endowment.'

At this time, actually 1692, the annual value of property as assessed for land tax was £236 15s. .... The reputed date of the Bowling Green Inn is 1693, though it may well have been serving refreshment for many years before the introduction of licensing. In 1695 'Window Tax' was imposed; the only building to show evidence of the way in which symmetry was maintained by dummy windows is Hough End Hall. In 1701 the tithes of the township were leased out, or 'farmed', by the Warden and Fellows of the Manchester Collegiate Church, but to whom is not recorded. The population in 1714 was 325, made up of sixty-five families, of whom fourteen were dissenters. Anthony Barlow (X), as a papist, was required in conformity with an Act of the first year of Geerge I, to register his estate, the yearly value of which he returned as £171 9s.

Briefly, in 1716, we find the Rev. John Thomas as curate; in 1717 Joseph Dale had taken over and was combining the curacy of Chorlton with that of Birch (Booker comments '. . . with no prospects of permanency') and the inhabitants of Chorlton were adding £10 each year to his stipend. Mr. Dale got involved in trouble at Didsbury between Lady Bland, the curate Thomas Wright and the Bishop of Chester. It concerned parochial income from land and was very involved.[67] In one of his letters to his Bishop, Mr. Wright, ever anxious to vindicate himself in the eyes of the Bishop, writes:

'Mr. Dale, he comes a preacher at Chorlton Church (after a mobbing way) to draw both my congregation after him, and by his fawning, insinuating ways, to take their affection off me to himself; there he comes and preaches without the consent of the fellows of Manchester, and (I presume) without your lordship's license.'

Three months later, in a further letter, dated 10th January 1720–21, the Lord Bishop of Chester is informed:

'My lord, I am persecuted and hunted like a partridge upon a mountain, yet I doubt not but when the truth appears, your honour will find these proceedings of Mr. Dale's and Mr. Broome's to be nothing but malice and roguery.'

and later:

'. . . Mr. Stratford said he had silenced Mr. Dale by your

lordship's order; but it proved nothing so; for he has preached ever since, sometimes at Chorlton Chapel, sometimes at Northen, which is but half a mile from me, and draws a many of my congregation after him.'

Apart from the rights and wrongs of the case it would appear that Mr. Dale was the loser. Mr. Wright seems to have retired from the incumbency in 1720–21, but a Thomas Wright, and it is by a strange coincidence if it is not the same man, was nominated by William Birch to 'my chapel at Birch' on 11th July 1720 and, on the same day, by the Warden and Fellows of Manchester to Chorlton Chapel.[68]

It would be reasonable to assume that the advantage of plurality of livings as a means of offsetting the smallness of the stipend was becoming increasingly obvious and no doubt this side-play between Mr. Dale and Mr. Wright was concerned with this rather than the main issue.

For the next quarter of a century we have no record of the minister at Chorlton, a period in which the endowment of the chapel was increased by £200 (1723) and Lady Bland gave a silver paten (1733) which, with the chalice she had given at her wedding, was to be used in the chapel and parish church for many years. Margaret Usherwood and Jane Gee in the following year gave a silver tankard. Who these two ladies were is not known but the present Whitelow Road is cut in part through what was known as the 'Gee Field' (more precisely the area where York Road runs into Whitelow Road) and Margaret Usherwood goes on record as the provider of the only charity restricted to the township of Chorlton. By her will dated 23rd August 1742, and proved at Chester 2nd April 1773 (she died 19th November 1748), Richard Broome, Nathaniel Gee, Jonathan Lowe and Samuel Bradshaw were charged with administering the residue of her estate in such a way as to allow the interest from its investment to provide for six poor children whose parents frequented Chorlton Chapel, with particular consideration for any whose surname was Warburton or Williamson. On selection each child was to be provided with a blue gown and blue cap, a pair of blue stockings, a shirt and a pair of shoes. Each child was to benefit from the charity for four years and was required to regularly attend Chorlton Chapel and sit in the places near the altar reserved for them. After two years they were to receive the same clothing as before and for the four years the 'schoolwages' for their instruction was to be paid. Boys were instructed in reading and writing, girls in reading and needlework, but funds would not always satisfy all the demands, consequently the number of children benefiting and the extent of their benefit varied according to the money available. It was customary for the trustees to invite new members when their number was reduced to two. From some time in the XIX century the charity became inoperative and the income was paid into the school fund. A stone commemorating the charity was sited in the aisle of the Old Church, probably where the beneficiaries could contemplate it when the sermon was dull, and though the church has been demolished the stone is still *in situ* at the time of writing.

The closing months of 1745 saw the troops of Prince Charles Edward, the 'Young Pretender' arrive in Manchester on their way south. As it had been a century before, the river Mersey was a strategic line. There was much play and counterplay designed to confuse the other side. The length of the river between Stockport and Flixton was a likely place for the Prince's crossing; Crossford Bridge between Stretford and Sale was demolished by the 'Liverpool Blues' on Government instructions—on leaving for the south the Prince issued a proclamation to the effect that he had given orders to repair the several bridges 'forthwith, particularly that at Crossford, which is to be done this night by his own troops. . . .' Even so the work and expense seems, from the Manchester Constables' Accounts (vol. III p. 22), to have been assumed locally. The temporary bridge was soon re-erected at the expense of the county.

As part of the subterfuge the Prince encamped his troops at several places along the Lancashire side of the river; a party camped in Chorlton on the slight rise bounded by Whitelow, Wilbraham and Brundretts Roads and High Lane. This area was known until very recently as Scots Hill (or Scotch hill) and it is perhaps this association which caused the house erected a century and a half later on the corner of Manchester Road and High Lane, to be known as Oban House.

All the evidence points to the main body of the Prince's army leaving on 1st December by way of Cheadle Ford for the south. A temporary bridge had been erected here but a small detach-

ment from Barlow Moor may have crossed by Barlow Ford
(whose site is now unknown unless it was the same as the ford
which existed a hundred yards or so south of Jackson's Boat), and
a diversionary party left Manchester by way of the temporarily
repaired Crossford Bridge. This latter went by way of Altrincham to join the main party near Macclesfield. It may be that
the party which camped at Chorlton can be identified with this
group. It would be sensible for them to camp overnight somewhere off the beaten track before moving on to the south, and
Chorlton was ideal from this point of view.

There is an old tale that a group of Stuart sympathizers
regularly met in the house on the site of the Jackson's Boat Inn
where they would toast 'The King' sitting round a table with a
bowl of water in the centre. When, on one occasion, a guest
remarked, knowing the sympathies of the gathering, that it was
not the toast he would have expected, the reply was 'Tush! are
we not drinking to the King over the water?' We have already
seen that there was suspicion of Stuart sympathy in the Barlow
family.[69] Obviously the local people did not like the troops or
their habits for they hid horses in Hough End Clough (and, no
doubt, elsewhere) to prevent their seizure by the army.[70]

The old Hough Hall was demolished in 1750 to make way
for Old Hall Farm (or Chorlton's Farm), but the moat remained
until the whole area was built up by Manchester Corporation
between the wars. The following year saw the Hough End
estates of the Mosleys, together with the Manorship of Withington sold to the Egertons of Tatton, and the Hulme estates, which
included a not inconsiderable amount of land in Chorlton, sold
to George Lloyd. So ended the ties with one of the two most
important local families.

The Rev. Oldfield became curate in 1754. He had been
librarian to Chetham's Library between 1726 and 1732, but
from whence he came to Chorlton is not known. He retired from
Chorlton in 1766, to be succeeded by the Rev. Richard Assheton
whose nomination leaves some doubt as to the possibility of a
Rev. Thomas Beeley being his immediate predecessor. It may
be that Mr. Beeley was a stipendiary curate, receiving a payment from the licensed holder of the office.

The Rev. John Salter followed Mr. Assheton in 1771,
followed as perpetual curate in 1789 by Joshua Brookes. Mr.

Brookes had been stipendiary curate from 1782 until his nomination to succeed Mr. Assheton, and resigned in 1791 on being appointed Chaplain of the Manchester Collegiate Church. Of Joshua Brookes much has been written. He is probably the most remarkable cleric of all time and could well justify a biography on his own. He was the eccentric son of an eccentric father and though there is a temptation to record here some of the anecdotes which are told of him, on the excuse that none are known which have a direct connection with his curacy at Chorlton, the reader is directed to other sources. Booker in 'History of the Chapels of Didsbury and Chorlton; Ellwood in his South Manchester Gazette series, Chapter XI; and Mrs. Linnaeus Banks's 'Manchester Man' will all help to fill in a background picture of this fascinating character.

By now the timber-framed chapel was life expired. It had stood the test of time and weather for two and a half centuries and it was decided to replace it with a new structure. Consequently the old building was closed and demolished in 1779 and the new building, of less aesthetic merit but more convenient red brick, was completed the following year. That this new building was a singularly long narrow building we know, for the alterations made to widen it in 1837 were clear to be seen by anybody who knew the 'old church', but no pictorial record of its initial form is known. It was in this building, newly built, that Joshua Brookes commenced his work in Chorlton.

The population return of 1774 shows the village to consist of 378 individuals in 75 families, an increase of only 53 individuals and ten families in the sixty years since the 1714 return. There were 71 houses to shelter the 75 families and we are given an interesting break-down of the ages: 147 under 15; 69 above 50; 17 above 60; 10 above 70, and two above 80.

Religious toleration had come as a result of the Act of 1689. Slowly the neighbouring conurbation of Manchester there had been a movement away from High-Church practices, at first epitomised in the activities of Lady Bland and the founding of St. Ann's Church, and moving even further away with the passing of the Toleration Act of 1689. The first non-conforming chapel to be built in Manchester was that at Cross Street in 1693. Methodism was introduced to the Manchester area sometime between 1733 and 1738 and a 'Methodist Society' was established shortly after this latter date. The first Methodist chapel was built in Birchin Lane, near High Street, in 1750. The reforming zeal of the movement caused its adherents to increase rapidly in numbers and soon the message was being carried outside the limits of the town. Ellwood asserts that it was first received in Chorlton about 1770 when a uniformed soldier and his supporters arrived on the Green. The soldier, standing on a large stone, delivered the first of the many Methodist sermons which have been delivered in the village since that time.

Before 1800 regular Methodist services were being held in Chorlton and a Methodist Society, albeit a scanty five in number, was in existence by the turn of the century. Early services were held in the homes of members, particularly in John Johnson's thatched cottage, on the site of the National Schools on the Green, Thomas Baguley's cottage in what is now Beech Road, and John Baguley's in St. Clement's Road. In summer the meetings were held in the barns belonging to Mrs. Higginbotham and Mrs. Joseph Chesshyre. The former building still stands helping to restrict the exit from the Green. The enthusiasm for the new form of religion continued to grow and increasingly there were occasions when all those wishing to attend service could not be accommodated. Jeremiah Brundrett, the elder, decided that if Methodism was to continue its growth, some more suitable permanent premises would have to be provided. To that end he gave a square of land in Beech Road and a not inconsiderable sum of money (for the time) to help provide a chapel. The site was that part of the present graveyard adjacent to the Trevor Arms Hotel, to the right of the path and between the road and the later building. The square building, small though it might seem from today's inspection of the ground, is said to have had a capacity of about 100 persons. Ellwood was able to draw on the memories of people very near the time and records that, in the manner common at the time, there was segregation of the sexes. The men sat on forms on the right and the women on the left, with a rail positioned down the centre to emphasise the division. Those who arrived late had to occupy a 'sinners' form' behind the door, but we are not told if segregation extended that far. No heating was provided and lighting was by candles. Worship was spartan in those days!

Singing was led by voices and an orchestra; three forms were reserved, the first for violins and clarionets, the second for flutes and male singers and the third, and top-most, for women singers who, again referring to Ellwood, had a piece of 'matting tacked on the wall as a protection from the damp'!—from which one may assume that this 'top-most' form was at the back of the chapel. Even in those early days of sparse population the Sunday services were soon being held in the morning and afternoon with a prayer meeting in the evening.

This chapel was first used about 1805 and almost from the beginning a Sunday School was held in connection with it. This was the earliest such school in the neighbourhood, predating the Church Sunday School by a number of years. After a few years Thomas Moores started collecting subscriptions in the village and was eventually able to purchase a plot of land and to build premises for the school on the corner of Whitelow Road and Beech Road. This building is probably, in its original form, what is now the Beech Inn, but the Methodists failed to convey either the land or the building legally into the care of trustees with the result that it was found possible for it to be offered for sale and bought over the heads of the Methodists. By what means this was done is not known but presumably it was by the original owner of the land, but thereafter the Methodist body found that they had to pay a yearly rent. James Renshaw, the so-called 'first Methodist in Chorlton' held a day school in the same building.

This state of affairs continued until some years after 1827, when the schools committee was given notice to vacate the premises, and the building was converted into dwellings. In the meantime the small chapel had proved insufficient for the need and in 1826 the same Jeremiah Brundrett who had been the instigator of the first chapel opened the way for a second and larger edifice by giving an additional plot of land and £20, to which his son, also Jeremiah, added £50. This younger Jeremiah set an example by spending all his spare waking moments working on the building. In July 1827, before the roof was added, a service was held in the shell. The completed building, formally opened in November 1827, cost £689 2s. 6d., and seated 274 persons of which 100 seats were free. Apart from some additional lighting over the pulpit by candles, oil was used to light the new building, and a stove provided the heating. There was a gallery provided with pews at one end and at first pews were only provided in the centre of the floor. As the congregation grew, additional pews were provided at the sides. A relic of the first chapel survived in the chapel doors which were utilised in the new building, and probably as much as possible of the materials of the old building was used in the new. In 1855 a second-hand organ was bought for £70 and lived to be incorporated into the third chapel in 1873. Gas, the ultimate luxury, was introduced for lighting in 1862.[71]

After the translation of Mr. Brookes to the Collegiate Church came the Rev. Nicholas Mosley Cheek. He seems to have played little part in the affairs of the chapel and his appointment of Roger Mashiter as stipendiary curate in 1796 and Samuel Stephenson in a similar capacity in 1801 (to 1807) suggests that he was one who appreciated the value of plurality of livings. Mr. Stephenson retained his post for the first two years of Mr. Cheek's successor, the Rev. George Hutchinson who, in due course, appointed George Holt, 'a literate person', in 1807 followed in turn by John Collins as stipendiary curate in 1812.

Between 1816 and 1833 Chorlton was, officially, in the care of the Rev. R. H. Whitelock who not only looked after this village but was also Vicar of Skillington in Lincolnshire, curate of St. Mark's, Cheetham (licensed 5th January 1816) and for good measure was postmaster of Manchester. There is no record of who did the work in Chorlton but it is unlikely that he had much time to spare and the reference to the provision of the first village school and master's house in 1817 as a result of a public subscription is without doubt a reference to the school, already mentioned, provided by the efforts of Thomas Moore and kept by James Renshaw.

James Renshaw was strict to the point of cruelty. He had but one leg and whilst the adults of the village valued his advice on most subjects, the scholars were ever ready to play him up. Each morning a boy was despatched to old Renshaw's thatched cottage (where Joel View now stands) to collect his breakfast of a quart jug of oatmeal porridge and a spoon. Ellwood describes how young Charles Brundrett was on one occasion deputed to throw the jug and its contents in the pond and bury the spoon. There is no record of the outcome when the schoolmaster stormed out of the school as a result of a 'tip-off' only to find that he was too late.

Mr. Whitelock died in August 1833 and was followed by the Rev. Peter Hordern, M.A., who combined the curacy with the office of librarian of Chetham's Library. He died, as had so many of his predecessors, in harness in March 1836. The income of the chapelry in 1835 was £103 per annum from £400 of private benefactions and £600 from Queen Ann's Bounty, which was invested in land. In the footsteps of Mr. Hordern came the Rev. John Morton, during those term of office the chapel was enlarged by the adding of side aisles with the insertion of cast-iron pillars, of very slender proportion, to support the roof where the original outside walls had been. In the enlarged building there were 521 sittings, of which 200 were free.

Mr. Morton also saw the Parish of St. Clement, Chorlton-cum-Hardy promulgated in the London Gazette in 1839 and an organ installed in 1842. Before the organ the congregation had been led by instrumental music, latterly by a violincello played by James Gresty of Martledge.

Mr. Morton died, also in office, in December 1842, to be followed by the Rev. William Birley, the first rector, whose nomination was dated 17th February 1843. Unlike some who had gone before him, Mr. Birley appears to have entered into parish work with enthusiasm, and it was under his guidance that funds were raised by subscriptions and grants of £150 from The Council on Education and £75 from the National Society to enable the first National School to be erected on the edge of the Green. The site, previously occupied by cottages, was conveyed to the Parish by George Lloyd of Stockton Hall, York. In 1848 Chorlton-cum-Hardy Parish was transferred to the new diocese of Manchester and two years later it was declared a district parish.

Priests often lived at some distance from their flock. Mr. Birley previous to the building of a rectory lived in a house on the corner of Upper Chorlton Road and Wood Road; prior to that he lived at Irwell View, Old Trafford. In 1859 Mr. Birley exchanged livings with the Rev. John Edmund Booth, M.A.

In the first half of the XIX century the population of the township grew from 513 in 1801 to 761 in 1851, not a particularly meteoric increase in view of what was to come. What can now be seen, in hindsight, as one of the last contacts with the old order was the visit of a military band with a sergeant marching at their head with drawn sword, beating up recruits for the army in the Napoleonic War in 1814. In 1815 the Scots Greys camped in the walled orchard of Hough End Hall (where now the Southern Hotel stands) preparatory to service at Waterloo. Of those of the village who enlisted, many never came back and a few were brought home for burial.

The nearness of the rapidly expanding town of Manchester began to have its effect and the outer ring of executive type houses approached nearer and nearer. In 1838 the old lane from the 'Flash' (later re-christened with the more euphemistic 'West Point') was straightened by Samuel Brooks to serve the housing complex he was building on Jackson's Moss which, in company with the Flash was thereafter to be known as Whalley Range. Ever ready to seize an opportunity, a gate (or 'bar') was erected at the Manchester end so that tolls could be exacted for its use. In order to prevent the improper use of the road without payment a gate, without a toll house, was erected in Wood Road. The charging of tolls ceased on 10th June 1896.

Even with this approach of her growing neighbour, Chorlton's secluded quietness was sufficient to make it attractive to the many who lived in the densely packed rows of dull terraced houses and they walked the six miles or more, there and back, to sample the country pleasures. Perhaps the attraction was the opportunity of engaging in or watching the sports and pastimes, sometimes illegal like cockfighting, in the meadows by the Bridge Inn (then called the 'Greyhound') and from which a hurried movement into Cheshire would herald the arrival of the Lancashire Law.

Jackson's Boat (though who was Jackson and when he first operated his boat is not known) was hauled across the river by means of a chain strung between two posts in the banks. It was replaced in 1816 by a wooden footbridge with three intermediate supports sunk into the bed of the river and modelled, it is said, on the old Blackfriars Bridge in Manchester. It was built by Samuel Wilton at a cost of £200, he being the owner of the inn at that time. Some years later the centre support was washed away by a flood but it continued to be used. A serious flood of December 1880 washed away the support on the Chorlton side and thus being made unsafe, John Brooks decided to re-place it with an iron girder bridge. The new bridge was to be opened on 14th October 1881, and by coincidence another heavy flood washed away the old bridge a few hours before the new one was due for opening.

Chorlton was increasingly aware of Manchester but it was still essentially an agricultural community, concerned with supplying food to Manchester's markets and enjoying a reputation for its apple orchards. Most old customs were still practised and the village constable still exercised his right to fine owners of animals found straying and impounded them in the pinfold—an oak stump enclosure adjacent to the church-yard. The land now occupied by the parish of St. Werburgh, that is part of Martledge and White Moss, was still sparsely populated. Dog House Farm, Old Dog House, Demesne Road indicated by their designations the extent of the old manorial holdings. Hobson's Hall, the South-west Manchester Cricket Club now occupies the site, was the most substantial building in the area.

The river was always a problem. The price of farming the ees was constant vigilance. Its behaviour was mercuric until industrial and domestic demands on the headwaters and improvements to the course reduced the extreme variations of flow and so safeguarded the banks from disintegration. There was always argument as to who was responsible for the repairs; in Urmston in 1641 there is a record of the election of 'Overseers of Water-courses' and 'Banklookers' whose duty it was to see that ditches, drains and river banks were maintained in good condition. In 1771, land between Gatley and Northenden was assessed at 9s. per acre towards the cost of strengthening the banks[72] and throughout the winter of 1840 the poor were employed in strengthening the banks at the expense of the land-owners who contributed to a common fund.[73] In 1770 an advertisement in 'The Mercury' newspaper gave notice of a meeting to be held at Altringham (*sic*) to assess damages to crops of farmers in Chorlton as a result of floods alleged to have been caused by the insufficient size of the canal bridge at Barfoot Hough damming up the water.

The building of the banks was a relatively simple matter. Stones and earth, reinforced with willow hurdles, brushwood, etc.[74] were thrown up in a bank on the land adjacent to, but a few yards from the channel, thus leaving a shelf. This provided a convenient though limited supply of material for repairs to the inside of the bank and an additional capacity to absorb flood water. Any material washed away could easily be replaced and as successive floods showed the need, additional height could be formed. If this constant repair was not maintained, the result could be spectacular.

In August 1779 a heavy flood broke the banks on the Sale side near Barfoot Hough Bridge and on the Chorlton side adjacent to where Chorlton Brook enters the Mersey. Fears were felt by the engineers of the recently completed Bridgewater Canal (1765) for the aqueduct across the flood plain and to relieve the strain in the event of future floods, an overflow channel was formed by improving the course of the Ousel or Kicketty Brook and a stone weir inserted in the bank. This was swept away by a summer flood of 1840 after which litigation resulted in the cost of repair being borne by the Bridgewater Trust £1,500, the Turnpike Commissioners £500, Thos. Jos. de Trafford £1,000 and Wilbraham Egerton £1,000. The cost of maintenance was at the same time decided as Bridgewater Trustees $\frac{1}{2}$. Thos. Jos. de Trafford $\frac{1}{4}$, and Wilbraham Egerton $\frac{1}{4}$. The new weir was built in 1841 and had William Cubitt, F.R.S., as its engineer.[75] The last time this weir served the purpose for which it was intended was 1915.

In July 1828 the banks were breached by a sudden flood near Barlow Hall and the meadows of Henry Jackson and John Cookson flooded so quickly that the horses had to be released from the shafts and stampeded to higher ground; nearer to Stretford George Lewis had gone with his horse and cart to the Ousel meadow for hay and was caught by the flood and had to stay there until the next day, while one of his friends, also from Stretford, climed into a birch tree and was next day rescued in an upturned butchers' 'turnel'(or scalding tub) used as a boat. One account describes how the haycocks were washed from Barlow Hall down to Barfoot Bridge and then, by a freak change in the wind, blown back almost to the spot from which they had started.

Surprisingly the river was clean enough to support fish until the 1850s. It is on record that a salmon was taken at Northen Eye in (c.) 1820 and Fletcher Moss remembered catching small fish as a boy 'like roach or dace'. That would be about 1850. A particularly succulent variety of small smelt appeared each year in large numbers.

The Industrial Revolution caused tremendous changes in the utilisation of land for growing food, many communities at the end of the XVIII and beginning of the XIX centuries were still farming largely on the basis of the wasteful 'strip system'. After the Napoleonic Wars and for some few years afterwards there was a spate of 'Land Enclosure Acts' designed to redraw completely the field patterns for more efficient and productive use. Chorlton was not affected, probably because the land under the Mosleys and Barlows had never been fully utilised. After the sale of the Mosley and Barlow estates the township was owned by the Egertons (who had bought the Hough End estates of the Mosleys and the Barlow estate) and George Lloyd's successors (who had bought the Hulme estates). These two landowners negotiated exchanges of plots to produce more efficient units and thereby largely achieved the same end but without an Act. Even so a scrutiny of the Tithe Map of 1845 shows in remarkable degree how, though farming units were convenient and compact, everybody had a share of the ees where the land was always at risk from floods. It is not hard to detect (as has already been pointed out), where the medieval strips were located.

Until the early years of the XIX century the government of the township was a survival of that practised through the manorial system from the Middle Ages. The first departure came with legislation to establish 'Boards of Guardians', primarily to take over responsibility for the poor and the homeless. The Poor Law Act was passed in 1834 and each sector of an area appointed 'guardians' to represent it. In 1837 Chorlton-cum-Hardy was incorporated into the Chorlton upon Medlock Poor Law Union administered by the Chorlton (upon Medlock) Board of Guardians.[76] Lancashire County administered some local functions (e.g. police) and certain officers, like the Overseer of Highways (for the Manor) were still appointed by the annual meeting of the Court Leet held at Michaelmas (28th October) each year in the Red Lion Inn at Withington. The last meeting of the Court Leet was in 1841 and amongst the officers elected were the traditional 'Ale Taster', 'Dog Muzzler' and 'Swine Looker'.

Church finances were based on a 'church rate' which was

levied on the annual value of all properties in the parish. Before Chorlton was a separate parish the rate (usually the figure was 10*d*. in the pound and authorized at the annual Vestry meeting) was collected by the Churchwardens and paid to the Parish Church of Manchester but afterwards it was payable to the new parish. There was always resentment over the payment and about 1850 the matter was brought to a head by non-payment on the part of certain individuals. The plea that the rate had been improperly levied, due to a technical error, was upheld and after that payment was accepted as voluntary.

Probably the most important monument to the Board of Guardians is the Nell Lane Hospital which in its original somewhat smaller and simpler form was the Withington Workhouse. When the Board was first formed there were but two workhouses in the twelve townships, one at Stretford with a capacity of 100 persons, and one at Gorton for thirty. Otherwise cottages were used for the poor and homeless and Chorlton's contribution was two thatched cottages overlooking the footpath through Hardy Croft (now Albermarle Road) and referred to in some sources as 'The Almshouses'. The Nell Lane institution was the second built by the Board (the first being opposite Holy Trinity Church, Stretford Road) and was designed to house 1,200 and have hospital accommodation for 200. In time, extensions were effected to increase on this.

This system of split responsibility ensured that the welfare of the individual suffered as the population increased and administration became more complex. Eventually necessity forced a change in local government but that is a story for the last chapter.

SPORTS, PASTIME and CUSTOMS

Fortunately Ellwood was able to talk to people whose memories went back to the end of the XVIII century and it is to these recorded memories that we owe our knowledge of the customs of the village. All recorded evidence points to a common form underlying customs on both sides of the river bank and extending through Stretford, Chorlton, Sale, Northen(den) and Didsbury. Behind most customs can be detected an element of begging and an integral part of most pastimes was an exploitation of cruelty. The pastimes enjoyed were generally baiting, fighting and the exercise of physical prowess.

Baiting was the setting of dogs against other animals, usually against bulls, badgers and bears, and by far the commonest and most popular was Bull Baiting. The bull-ring was set in a considerable stone block which was situated at the church end of the Green, a few yards from where the telephone kiosk now stands. The bulls were hired by the landlords of the inns, particularly the Horse & Jockey and the Bowling Green. The hiring out of animals of repute was a lucrative occupation of certain individuals in the neighbourhood, of whom James Moores, a butcher of Manchester, was one, and in the course of walking the bulls to Chorlton and back there was many an incident which left dead dogs in the ditches and hedgerows.

The bulls, rejoicing in fanciful names like 'Young Fury' (which was the son of 'Old Fury'), were tethered to the ring by a chain roughly twenty yards long. The dog was unleashed ('slipped') at the bull and thereafter it was a cruel test of experience. An experienced bull would try to take the dog on its horns, throw it high into the air and by the fall break its back. The crowd were not above helping by trying to break the dog's fall. The dog tried to seize the bull by the nose and hold on until the beast came to a stand. This was termed 'pinning the bull'. For fair play (!) only one dog was slipped at a time.

Bear baiting was less common, bears being in much shorter supply than bulls. The rules, if as such they can be termed, were not dissimilar to those of bull baiting but with an experienced bear the results could be much more bloody. Again, fair play was observed:

> One dog, one bear,
> Two dogs, ain't fair!

as the rhyme had it.

Probably the cruelist sport was Badger Baiting. In Chorlton this was latterly practised at a public house sometime known as the Black Horse (and possibly at one time as the Bull's Head) at Lane-end—that is where Sandy Lane, High Lane and Barlow Moor Road converge. At one period the house was kept by Thomas Chorlton and John Williamson kept the badgers in his stable in High Lane. The badger, for the contest, was in a box with an opening on the top and another at the other end, being, in a crude sort of way, an approximation of its burrow. The dog was introduced into the box through the end opening and immediately a lively fight developed. From time to time the dog was pulled out by the tail but the badger was at a decided disadvantage and usually the dog was the victor.

Cock fighting was the most popular of such contests and, probably because of the personal involvement, was considered to be much superior. The same enthusiasm, but without the cruelty, is evident today in the whippet racing enjoyed by the miners of the North-east. The 'cock-clod' was under a large tree at Barlow Range at the Lane-end. The specially bred birds were additionally armed with steel spurs strapped to their legs and were brought hooded to the 'main'. Because of the ease with which the birds could be moved from place to place, the sport was still followed in the seclusion of the meadows long after it had been declared illegal; indeed it is still practised in the more remote parts of these islands.[77]

Of dog fighting little can be said, there was little other than shear cruelty involved. Only those with the basest feelings participated in these sports, but surely the lowest were those who deliberately promoted dog fights.

In 1835 an Act of Parliament outlawed most of these pastimes. The last recorded bull-baiting in Chorlton was at the village wakes of that year.

The more acceptable sports were prize-fighting, foot-racing and up-and-down-wrestling, this latter being similar to Cumberland style, and these were usually held in the meadows but so much drunkenness and unruly behaviour attended them that the forces of law and order were sometimes constrained to act. At the first sight of the law everybody, spectators and participants alike, would scurry across the bridge (which had been conveniently left open) into Cheshire where they could conclude their unfinished business outside the 'Lancashire-law'.

Horse racing was followed in the XVI century, traditionally the site being a field known as the 'Scaffold Field' now a part of Chorlton Park. This field can be more accurately defined as being the area north of the path in line with the front entrance to Hough End Hall, and occupied by the schools and the bowling-greens. It is said, (by Ellwood who seems to be the only source and the one frequently quoted), that there was a small hillock in the field which served as a grandstand, and that the races were later transferred to Kersal Moor, so establishing

Chorlton as the original home of the Manchester race course. There is nothing known of a scaffold existing, let alone being used.

These sports and pastimes were generally confined to the three holiday periods of Easter, Whit and the Village-wakes, but with the growth of Manchester the village became the week-end haunt of the artisans. With Sunday as their non-working day and the day when one could only buy intoxicants if a bona fide traveller (having travelled more than three miles) they satisfied all their interests by walking to Chorlton and the inn-keepers of the village and others were quick to provide the necessary attractions. The official distance from All Saints to the corner of St. Clement's Road and High Lane was 3m. 775 yards.[78]

The principal sport enjoyed by the villagers, to be pursued when the working day was over, was undoutedly bowls. Most of the public houses had a green attached or near at hand and the Bowling Green Hotel and the Bridge Inn still retain theirs. That of the Horse & Jockey disappeared many years ago but when the Lloyd Platt Hotel was built in 1870 a green was considered an essential part of the amenities. By this time private bowling clubs were also providing facilities.

The customs of the village were of two types. There were those which involved the presentation of some form of entertainment for which a reward was expected, and those which meted out a rough sort of justice, often cruel but intended to indicate that the recipient had offended against the standards of propriety.

The former group was large. They started at Easter with the performing of mumming plays which, having in recent years enjoyed considerable popularity, require little description. Few have not heard of 'Bold Slasher's' fight with 'St. George', or of 'Open The Door', 'Black Morocco Knight', 'Doubt' as well as the more prosaic 'Doctor' and 'The Devil'. Always the theme was the triumph of good over evil and the whole thing is remarkable for its antiquity and widespread observance. The 'Doctor' carried a bottle of physic and a stick, the others carried swords with St. George often riding a hobby horse.

The party (in view of the strenuous nature of the performance it would be from the younger men) dressed up in any suitable finery and started their rounds at dawn on Good Friday. The performance was regarded as the high spot of the year by the children who tagged along from performance to performance, seemingly never to get tired of watching the final fight in which St. George always vanquished Bold Slasher and the powers of evil. A 'lady' with a basket, always a man dressed as a woman, accompanied the mummers and collected the gifts of eggs, cakes, gingerbread, liquor or money given by those to whom the show was presented.

The older men of the village waited until Easter Monday when they disguised themselves with masks over their faces and stuffed straw under the white shirts they wore tied at the bottom. One of the party was covered with a horse-cloth and carried a horse's head on the end of a short pole. This was cunningly contrived so that the jaw could be made to snap by the manipulation of a lever and great fun was had by snapping at anybody who came near. The girls usually loved it and would scream for somebody to protect them. Sometimes there developed a considerable amount of horse-play with everybody laying about with bladders on sticks. The 'horse' was usually known as Old Hob.

These customs were observed over the Easter period. On Easter Sunday it was the practice to exchange eggs, often gaily coloured with distinctive patterns, to commemorate the Resurrection but this seems to have fallen into disuse in Chorlton at an early date. On Easter Monday and Tuesday was witnessed the custom of 'lifting' or 'heaving', again probably a reference to the Resurrection. The men lifted the women and on the Tuesday the women lifted the men. A small group would wander round the village and on seeing a victim, two members would grasp wrists to form a 'chair' and coming up behind would contrive to make him (or her) sit in the chair. There would follow a brief and vigorous period of lifting before being released. Ellwood records the story of a parson passing through a Lancashire town on Easter Tuesday and having to pass a few hours at an inn was surprised when a group of buxom wenches rushed into his room 'to lift him'. After the surprised cleric had elucidated the nature of the ceremony he purchased his immunity for a half-a-crown.[79]

The next festivities were concerned with May Day. In the period between mid-April and the last day of that month small groups of men, with such musical instruments as they could muster, visited the homes of farmers and the gentry to sing May Carols. Two of these were sung, the 'Old May Song' and the 'New May Song'.[80]

There was a widespread belief that sparrows were harmful to crops and in an attempt to reduce their number the village constable paid $\frac{1}{2}d$. for each sparrow's head or young spug, and when the birds were particularly numerous, $\frac{1}{4}d$. for each egg. The money was paid out of the income of the office of constable. When John Brundrett of Oak House Farm was constable, several youths passing by and seeing a number of heads recently paid for and thrown on the manure heap, collected them and received from John the appropriate payment. Sir Bosdin T. Leech in 'Old Stretford' tells a similar story but records that from the numbers presented it rapidly became evident that a fraud was being worked. In the Stretford Vestry Minutes for 26th October 1836 it is minuted that '. . . a halfpenny each be paid for sparrow heads taken within the Township and the expense be defrayed out of the Highway rate but that the constables first take them.' Eventually more enlightened views obtained.

The great event of the year was the village wakes. In Chorlton this was the week following the third Sunday in July, the Sunday being the day observed as the feast of St. Clement to whom the church was dedicated. The celebrations began on the previous day when new rushes to cover the floor of the church were brought through the village to the church, those which had served for the past year (!) were swept out and the new ones laid. In course of time this became a spectacle in its own right and while we have no specific knowledge of the ceremony of 'Rush Bearing' in Chorlton, or the date when it ceased, there are records of that at Didsbury in Fletcher Moss's works. 'Fifty Years of Public Work' includes photographs of the Didsbury Rush Carts of 1882 and 1911, which was the last occasion. Morris Dancers, musicians and large numbers of 'followers' accompanied the cart. In Chorlton a link existed until recent years in the annual procession of witness of the Sunday School but when this finished it marked the end of an association which went back to the very early days of the church in the township.

Wakes Sunday saw most villagers spending the morning in church (though there seems to have been doubt sometimes of the nature of their attendance) and in the afternoon there were games and sports including all those previously described. Peddlers were attracted and sold all manner of fancy wares, occasionally religious or quasi-religious performances were presented and open-house was observed everywhere. It was a time for visiting old friends and renewing ties which had been broken.

After the wakes there was little time for anything other than the harvest and by the time that was safely gathered in the winter was nigh. The villagers allowed themselves to celebrate the deliverance of Parliament by the building of a bonfire for which the village constable was expected to provide a quantity of fuel. Probably the value of the fire lay in the opportunity it provided to get rid of the waste of the autumn. Ellwood in his enquiries discovered that when the constable would not (or could not) provide material, it was usual for the villagers to take what they could from around his house. When Thomas Cookson was the constable he refused to honour the old custom, so the enraged locals not only took his fence, his barn doors and everything that they could move which would burn, they also ranged the village collecting from other sources. This pilfered material was built round a felled tree trunk outside the Horse & Jockey and the resulting fire was seen for many miles. In its glare the weather-cock on the church could be clearly seen. On the following morning John Turner collected three barrow loads of old hinges, fastenings, nails, latches and other iron!

Strangely there seems no custom peculiar to Christmas but there would be a break in the long cold dark winter until the days began to lengthen and Easter came round again.

Justice in the village was simple, and for parochial matters was probably dealt with locally because it was either too much trouble to refer to it the manorial court or it was of a kind outside the jurisdiction of that court. The village constable had defined local responsibilities, originally being the holder of an office under the Court Leet of the Manor, but latterly he was elected by the villagers. Amongst his duties was responsibility for the village pinfold. From the owner of each animal found straying he was permitted to collect 1s. or if it was not claimed within three days could sell 'to defray expenses'. The money collected was used in a variety of ways, poor relief and the payment for sparrow heads being but two.

The qualifications for office of constable was that he should be between 25 and 55 years of age, resident in the parish (of Manchester until the formation of the parish of Chorlton-cum-Hardy) and be rated to the relief of the poor to the extent of at least £4 per year. The election was held at the annual vestry meeting. In 1822 Sir Robert Peel, as he was to become, was appointed Home Secretary and in this capacity instituted a regular police force—for many years to rejoice in the name of peelers. For a time there were regular police and village constables side by side and the first regular policeman to be stationed in Chorlton was P.C. Gilpin about 1840. The appointment of parish constables ended at the vestry meeting of 1872 when the last holder of the office was appointed.

By law every village had to have stocks in which wrongdoers could be subjected to public humiliation. In Chorlton it would seem that these were situated adjacent to the pinfold. There is nothing recorded of any of the other punishment fixtures such as a ducking-stool, pillory, etc., and it is unlikely that they ever existed in the township.

A form of rough justice termed 'Riding the Stang' was practised in Chorlton as well as all the other communities in this part of Lancashire. As a means of expressing displeasure it caused a great measure of ill-feeling, and it was a happy day when, about 1840, it finally fell into disuse. It depended very much on the rabble-rousing of a ring-leader and it can be assumed that when there was no such moving spirit, the custom was largely disregarded.

The punishment was used when somebody was unfaithful to their spouse, when a man allowed himself to be henpecked (in the eyes of the village a serious thing) or when the husband beat his wife. The villagers would take whatever they could find which would make a loud and discordant noise and gather outside the home of the offender. The ringleader often sat in a chair which was carried by some of the crowd, or was sometimes seated in a cart drawn by a number of the mob. Pots, pans, warming-pans, kettles, bugles, cow horns, anything that would make a noise contributed to the discordant din. Shouts of shame, hisses, yells, were hurled at the unfortunate victim and after making their point, they marched off through the village proclaiming the reason for the exhibition wherever there was somebody to hear it.[81]

Another custom, in some eyes cruel, was that of fixing a besom (or yard brush) to the chimney of the home of a man whose wife had left him, indicating thereby that there was half a bed to spare.

In Ellwood's record of his inquiries into old customs there are several which he does not mention. As they were generally observed in this district, it is probable that they were also observed in Chorlton. Perhaps they had fallen into disuse before the time of Ellwood's informants.

Considering the rural character of Chorlton, it is surprising, but there were some who were too poor to have eggs to eat unless they were stolen or taken from the hedgerows where some hen was laying away. Some of the children who paraded with their baskets at Easter begging for eggs would otherwise never taste one. If the family was too poor to have the traditional dish of eggs on Easter Day, they would have 'furmety'—wheat stewed in the oven until the kernl swells and splits the outer bran. Another traditional dish at Easter was 'tansy pudding', tansy being a bitter herb.[82]

In Withington the eve of May Day was known as 'Mischief Night', suggesting that a spirit of fun was abroad in readiness for the festivities of the morrow. Ellwood makes no mention of dancing round the maypole. The writer remembers, as a small child shortly after the first world war, that in the 'Infants' Room' of the Old School on the Green there stood a large portable maypole. It was much too big for any of the infants, it was old and the ribbons no longer had any claim to freshness, indeed it was never used, in his memory, and in an age when such apparatus for schools was unprovided (slates were still used on occasions to eke out paper supplies) it was a mystery. It might have been that with the enclosure of the Green by Mr. Wilton. . . ? Perhaps!

Reference has already been made to Rush Bearing and the part the Morris Men played in the ceremony. These traditional dancers also made an appearance on May Day, at Easter as an accompaniment to the mummers and at other occasions as the opportunity presented itself.

The poor went 'souling' on All Soul's Day (2nd November). This is thought to have been a pre-Reformation practice but had degenerated into yet another excuse for the poor to beg. In this case it was for 'soul cakes', traditional round flat cakes with spice seasoning. In like manner the Feast of St. Thomas (21st December) was used as an excuse to beg, in this case for wheat (for Christmas) but latterly, again, for anything available. The custom was referred to as 'going a-tummusing'. Both these customs seem to have lasted until the last century.

Until the early XIX century it was a duty of churchwardens to 'fetch' people who had illegitimate (or 'base-born') children to do penance in the church. These people were known as 'light-o'-loves' and did their penance standing facing the congregation, wrapped in a sheet, during a church service. Fletcher Moss records a case at Northen (den) church and Ellwood records that the last person to do penance in Chorlton was Mary Crowther at the end of the XVIII century but he does not specify her offence.

THE TITHE AWARD MAP, 1845

Fortunately the Tithe Award Map of 1845 is available to us, together with the Book of References. A copy of this map, in reduced scale, and with added information from other contemporary sources is appended. Inspection will quickly reveal the extent to which the township was an agricultural community.

The low-lying land bordering the river and that in the area of 'The Isles' was almost entirely meadow, the remainder was arable or devoted to orchards or small holdings. These latter were referred to in the Book of References as 'gardens'. In 1845 there were 490 acres of arable land, 680 acres of meadow and pasture and 10 acres of woodland.

After the sales of the Mosley and Barlow estates, ownership was largely divided between the Lloyds and the Egertons. In 1845, again, of the 1,279 acres 2 roods 35 perches (which the Ordnance Survey estimated was the area of Chorlton-cum-Hardy) Wilbraham Egerton owned 887a. 2r. 12p. and George Lloyd 231a. 1r. 18p. This left 160 a. 3r. 5p. between 21 remaining owners of which James Holt and Charles Walker (of Longford House) held the most. Fourteen owned single plots, usually described as 'house and garden'. In the early years of the XIX century much exchanging of plots between the Lloyd and Egerton interests was directed towards forming more efficient farming units, thus largely effecting the same result as was elsewhere obtained by a 'Land-Enclosure' Act.

Farms were convenient, compact units but, perhaps not surprisingly, the old principle followed in the distribution of 'strips' whereby everybody had some of the bad as well as the good was still evident. Even John Cookson, whose holdings were compactly arranged round his Dark Lane Farm (which the present-day Clarendon Rd. W. bisected) had his holding in these.

Reference has already been made to the 'Scaffold Field'. The 6 in. Ordnance Survey of 1848 shows a small mound in the garden of Brookfield House, the house in Chorlton Park, described as 'Observatory' (map ref. $823\frac{1}{2}931\frac{1}{2}$). The whims of the early tenants of Brookfield are not recorded but in the late XVIII and early XIX century it was usual for 'gentlemen' to occupy their time in studying the 'arts and sciences'. Perhaps somebody, having seen the mound, produced an explanation, the wish being father to the thought.

. . . .

With the mid-eighteen hundreds, Chorlton slipped imperceptibly out of her centuries-old isolation and into a new and different age. . . .

NOTES

[31] On a gold ground with a horizontal black bar, three eagles in black with wings and legs outstretched. In heraldry known as 'displayed'.

[32] The arms were perpetuated as those of the Manor of Withington and adopted ultimately, probably without authority, by the Withington Local Board on its formation. On the demise of that body the arms fell into disuse until eventually adopted as the badge of the Burnage Grammar School.

[33] Nine miles n. of Burton-on-Trent and 8 miles w. of Derby, lying about 3 miles s. of the A52 Derby–Ashbourne road.

[34] Booker H.C.D.C., p. 130.

[35] The river Severn was the great commercial highway from the Midlands, and Bridgnorth was the most convenient shipment point for the Wolverhampton district. This marriage suggests that ties between the various branches of the family were strongly maintained.

[36] Booker H.C.D.C., p. 131 *et seq.* for full text.

[37] £30.

[38] The area about the south end of Deansgate. Alport Lodge seems to have been sited approximately where Knott Hill Market was later to stand. Alport Park, later Alport Town, was where Central Station was later to be sited and the bottom length of Deansgate was known as Alport Lane until the last century. In 1598 William, Earl of Derby, granted Nether Alport 'with the lodge thereon and certain fields called Over Alport, together with other lands which lay between the pales of the said park and the Irwell. . . .' to Sir Randle Brereton (Reilly, History of Manchester, p. 125).

[39] This 'Hough' was probably the one near Wilmslow. Chollerton and Chorleton were probably distinguished by '—with Hardy' and '—Row'. Turve Moss = Turf-moss, now Turn Moss.

[40] Booker H.C.D.C., p. 140 et seq. for full text.

[41] Rolleston is about 2 miles n. of Burton-on-Trent and only a few miles south of Longford (see 33).

[42] Booker H.C.D.C., p. 149 et seq.

[43] Booker quotes: '. . . descend to his cousin Edward Mosley, son of Edward Mosley of Hulme, Esq., and great grandson of Anthony Mosley of Ancoats Esq., the younger brother of Sir Nicholas Mosley Knt., . . .' This should obviously refer to 'son of Oswald Mosley', not Edward.

[44] Booker H.C.D.C., p. 162 et seq. for text.

[45] He was elected in the first parliament assembled by Edward VI and served throughout that reign and the first four parliaments of Queen Mary.

[46] Booker. Sir Richard St. George was Norroy King of Arms. Leonard Smedley probably kept him aware of changes which were of heraldic concern in the district.

[47] He fought at Flodden and built the Stanley Chapel in the Collegiate Church of Manchester. See 'Blessed Ambrose Barlow' by Dom Julian Stoner, O.S.B.

[48] Stanley Papers, pt. II, p. 212, Chetham Society.

[49] Booker H.C.D.C., p. 256 et seq.

[50] In some families it was the custom to send young sons to serve in a menial capacity in the household of a relative or close friend. This was probably to teach humility and service in a way which would not be possible in one's own family.

[51] The Leghs of Adlington.

[52] Sir Urian married Margaret Trafford whose brother married Lady Mildred Cecil, whose son, Sir Cecil Trafford, married Penelope, daughter of Sir Humphrey Davenport and grand-daughter of Lady Davenport in 1628. Notwithstanding the influence of her husband's family, Penelope brought up her children as Catholics. One of them, also named Penelope, married John Downes.

[53] Said to have been brought on by worry over the news that someone he loved greatly was resolved to do something very wrong which would lead to the ruin of many souls.

[54] Ampleforth Journal, Vol. LXXV, Pt. III, pps. 392-394.

[55] It has been stated that it was Eccles church and Wardley Hall which were involved, and a Mr. Risley, a Justice of the Peace as instigator. The facts as known support the account given here.

[56] Pilgrimages to Old Homes, 1906, Fletcher Moss.

[57] Booker, H.C.D.C., pps. 282-283.

[58] Booker, H.C.D.C., p. 285 et seq.

[59] Eccles 1192, Flixton and Prestwich 1291. These three were not in the parish of Manchester. The chapel at Denton, like Didsbury, a dependent of the Manchester church was built 1331.

[60] Salfordshire Wapentake Court Rolls for 1326 contain an entry of iij^d to be paid by William, the clerk of Stretford. 'Manorial Records' Crofton, H.S.C. I, p. 48.

[61] Booker, H.C.D.C., p. 240.

[62] A copy was presented to the churchwardens of Chorlton-cum-Hardy by the Rev. J. Clarke, rector of Stretford and rural dean, on 6th December 1855. —Ellwood.

[63] Booker, H.C.D.C., p. 303.

[64] Booker, H.C.D.C., p. 311 et seq., quotes a great deal of the evidence. The rather extended reference given here provides an excellent insight into local politics of the time.

[65] Booker, H.C.D.C., p. 314 et seq.

[66] By inference from Booker, Crofton and Ellwood, it was likely that it was Edward Richardson, B.A. He was a pious man and competent scholar but the fact that he was granted a licence to be a Presbyterian teacher on 2nd May 1672, in the house of Robert Mort of Little Hilton (Hulton?), casts doubt on the validity of the assumption. Crofton, H.C.S. I, pps. 67/68.

[67] See Booker, H.C.D.C., p. 38 et seq., for the full story.

[68] Booker, H.B.C., p. 152.

[69] According to the 'Manchester Journal' a club of Manchester Jacobites met at the inn. Dr. John Byrom and Colonel Townley were two of the members, the latter swore heartily to the annoyance of the former and it is suggested that it was at one of these meetings that Dr. Byrom delivered his poetic reproof to the Colonel:

> O that the muse might call without offence,
> The gallant soldier back to his good sense!
> His temp'ral field so cautious not to lose,
> So careless quite of his eternal foes!
> Soldier, so tender of thy Prince's fame!
> Why so profuse of a superior name?
> For the King's sake, the brunt of battle bear,
> But for the King of king's sake, do not swear.

[70] Crofton, H.S.C. I, p. 11 et seq., I. Million, H. D., Fletcher Moss 'Didsbury in the '45' and Ellwood.

[71] A very complete description of the early years of Wesleyan Methodism appears in Ellwoods' articles in the South Manchester Gazette, 1885, chapters XV to XVIII.

[72] Fletcher Moss, 'Didsbury', p. 69.

[73] Kenneth Whittaker (H. W., p. 8) refers to the existence of a 'River Banking Company' in Didsbury in 1830, but Ivor Million H. D., makes no reference to it.

[74] Known in Stretford as 'Yortin', probably a dialect variant of 'yard' = a stick or rod. Crofton, H.S.C., I p. 32.

[75] Crofton, H. S. C. I, p. 30 et seq.

[76] Formed January 1837 with 11 townships. Chorlton-cum-Hardy was admitted March 1837. Various changes were made in its constituent townships over the years. See Ellwood, S. M. G., chapters XX and XXI.

[77] A good photograph of a gamecock appears on p. 92 of 'Fifty Years of Public Work in Didsbury'. Fletcher Moss.

[78] Authorized Hackney Carriage Distance Table. 1887 ed.

[79] Ellwood, S. M. G., chapter VIII.

[80] As the words of the two songs as sung in this neighbourhood are extant, it may be of interest to record them. They appear in 'Ballads and Songs of Lancashire' by John Harland, 1865. There was a measure of extemporising to suit local characters of the moment.

THE OLD MAY SONG

The second and fourth lines are the same in each verse except the last.

1   All in this pleasant evening together come are we,
     For the summer springs so fresh, green, and gay;
     We'll tell you of a blossom that buds on every tree,
     Drawing near to the merry month of May.

2   Rise up the master of this house, put on your chain of gold,
     We hope you're not offended, (with) your house we make so bold.

3   Rise up the mistress of this house, with gold along (upon) your breast,
     And if your body be asleep, I hope your soul's at rest.

4   Rise up ye little children, and stand all in a row,
     We should have called you one by one, but your names we do not know;

5   Rise up the little infant, the flower of the flock,
     The cradle that you do lay in, it stands upon a rock;

6   Rise up, the fair maid of this house, put on your gay gold ring,
     And bring to us a can of beer - the better we shall sing;

7   God bless this house and harbour, your riches and your store,
     We hope the Lord will prosper you, both now and evermore,

8   So now we're going to leave you in peace and plenty here,
     We shall not sing you May again until another year,

9   Fair Flora in her prime, down by yon riverside,
     Where the fields and the meadows they are green,
     Where little birds are singing, sweet flowers they are springing,
     And summer springs so fresh, green, and gay,
     Drawing near to the merry month of May.

THE NEW MAY SONG (also called 'The Basiers')
The basier is the local name for the 'auricula'.

1   Come and listen awhile unto what we shall say
     Concerning the season, the month we call May;
     For the flowers they are springing, and the birds they do sing,
     And the basiers are sweet in the morning of May.

2   When the trees are in bloom and the meadows are green,
     The sweet-smelling cowslips are plain to be seen,
     The sweet ties of nature, which we plainly do say,
     For the basiers are sweet in the morning of May.

3   All creatures are deemed, in their station below,
Such comforts of love on each other bestow;
Our flocks they're all folded, and young lambs
    sweetly do play,
And the basiers are sweet in the morning of May.

4   So now to conclude with much freedom and love,
The sweetest of blessings proceeds from above;
Let us join in our song, that right happy may we be,
For we'll bless with contentment in the morning of May.

The musical notation appears in Chambers's 'Book
of Days'.

[81] In Stretford the offenders were put on a gate or cart, if they could be caught, and pelted, ill-used and ducked in a convenient pond. The finale was the burning of an effigy. See 'Old Stretford' by Sir Bosdin T. Leech.

[82] Tansy (tanacetum) is a native British herb with feathery green leaves and small golden-yellow flowers. Its use at Easter is symbolic of the command at the Paschal feast.

Martledge, prob. c. 1885. Old Cottages between Warwich Road and Selbourne Road. (comm. p.c. 'Renaud' ref. 320).

Wilbraham Road from the Barlow Moor Road crossing looking towards the railway bridge. c. 1900. (W. H. S. and S. 'Grosvenor Series').

Holt Croft where the United Services Club is now sited. (comm. p.c. ref. 364).

Hymes Cottages, Hardy Croft, the path on the right is now Albermarle Road. c. 1880. (Published in the Wesleyan Bazaar Handbook 1895.)

Cow Lane, which ran between Edge Lane and the clay pit (Nicholas Road). The lower end became Hampton Road, about 1900. (Neil's Series).

Beech Road, c. 1895, looking towards Barlow Moor Road from Cross Road. Note the cottage projecting into the road opposite the site of the later Reynard Road. (source unknown).

Chorlton Priory about 1895. This stood where Priory Avenue now is and served as a religious house, 1890-1900 (photo. the late C. E. Jones).

A Fine Body of Men. Chorlton's Police Force standing on the steps of the Beech Road Police Station, c. 1922. (courtesy

Chapter Four

THE LAST HUNDRED YEARS

If a definite date had to be offered for Chorlton's transfiguration, it would, without doubt, be 20th July 1849—for on that day the Manchester South Junction and Altrincham Railway opened for business. Chorlton was at last within reasonably easy reach of Manchester and the event caused not only a population explosion but a complete fragmentation of the township. The close knit form of the community was destroyed as an ever increasing tide of strangers settled in.

This last chapter must, of necessity, be very much a patchwork of largely unconnected material. Since the cause of it all was the rapid ease of communications, it is proper that we start there. . . .

THE DEVELOPMENT OF LOCAL TRANSPORT

Prior to 1781 when the Duke of Bridgewater introduced his own 'most elegant' boats, on his Navigation through Stretford, the people of Chorlton made their own way to Manchester as best they could. Stage coaches stopped at the Angel Inn at Stretford but there would be few Chorltonians who would have the desire or the money to use the service. The canal provided the first public service to Manchester's Castlefield Wharf or to Liverpool at, initially, a fare of 1*d.* per mile. Slow though this method of travel was, it was more comfortable than the coach and at least as fast. Fares varied somewhat according to the accommodation, and the timetable depended on the times of tides in the Mersey Estuary.

The first competitor came in the early years of the XIX century when Massey's two-horse omnibuses started to operate between Altrincham and Manchester. A comfortable waiting room (we are told) was established at the Angel Inn at Stretford and prospective passengers were 'invited to make their way thither'. In the early years the fare from Stretford to Manchester was 1*s.* but, about 1845, Thornton's omnibus from Flixton began to ply via Stretford to be followed shortly by a similar venture by Emanuel Birkbeck. Competition forced down the fares to 6*d.*, the Canal imposing the same charge.

The opening of the railway in 1849 changed the situation at a stroke. It was now convenient for the princes of industrial and commercial Manchester to live in the pleasant suburbs, of which Stretford was but one. Edge Lane, previously a lonely country road, was quickly sold off in plots and fine new houses erected. When the part of the lane within Stretford was built up, the speculators moved into Chorlton and ribbon development crept nearer and nearer the Green. Whilst the last of these houses between Wilbraham Road and the boundary was only recently demolished, most of them (like Rye Bank House for instance) went many years ago. The more recent examples down to St. Clements Road are for the most part still standing though their role as family houses has been changed and even their coach houses have been turned into flats. They still retain many characteristic features and some still possess the wheel guide blocks outside the gates to prevent the polished brass rims of the carriage wheel hubs from scrawping the posts.

Chorlton started to reach out towards Stretford, and Stretford started to take an increasing interest in Chorlton. The Stretford Gas Company extended its main along Edge Lane in 1862 and John Greenwood's 'bus from the Greyhound at Flixton to Stretford station was from time to time extended through to Chorlton.

Meanwhile a direct service between Chorlton and Manchester by the way of the Flash (West Point) had been established. At first the service operated on Sundays, presumably in the summer, for the conveyance of those seeking the rural pleasure of Chorlton. This service of Christopher Batty's gave way to a regular service operated by Mr. Standring. This operated in the morning and evening, with occasional journeys through the day, from 23rd May 1864 but it was not long before the demand was answered with a two-hourly service throughout the day. In 1871 the Manchester Carriage Company acquired Mr. Standring's interest in the service and under the new owners the service became hourly with an additional service at 8-30 in the morning. Following the opening of Chorlton station on the Manchester South District line on 1st January 1880, the 'bus service was withdrawn in the February.[83]

The Manchester South District line was a typical product of the railway war. Originally intended as a link between Cornbrook and Heaton Mersey in the Cheshire Lines Committee's system, it was actually built by the Midland Railway on its own. Chorlton station had the same character as the other Midland stations like Withington and Didsbury, but upon the Manchester, Sheffield and Lincolnshire Railway constructing their line from Guide Bridge to Chorlton Junction through Fallowfield, the section from Chorlton Junction to Cornbrook was transferred to the Cheshire Lines with effect from 1st October 1891. This was the date of opening the section from Chorlton Junction to Fallowfield, the remainder to Guide Bridge was opened 2nd May 1892. The constituent companies of the Cheshire Lines were the Midland, Great Northern and Manchester, Sheffield & Lincolnshire Railways.

It was intended that the section through Chorlton should be four tracked and land on the east side was reserved for this purpose. Even when St. Werburghs Road Bridge was rebuilt in the 20's an arch for the additional tracks was provided, but in the last few years much of this strip has been sold for housing. The passenger services to Guide Bridge were withdrawn on 5th July 1958 and those through Didsbury 1st January 1967. Later the line through Didsbury was closed to all traffic and the track removed while the Fallowfield line was reduced to single-line working. Remotely controlled colour lights replaced the old semaphore signalling and the Junction signal box ceased to be operative.

The opening of the station largely arrested the development of the village towards Stretford, the builders turned their attention towards Martledge and soon a 'new village' was springing up.

In 1869 Wilbraham Egerton had cut a new road from Edge Lane, not far from the Stretford boundary, to Fallowfield, to open up large areas of his land for building.[84] This new road utilised a section of the 'Manchester Road' and thereafter the latter existed in two separated sections. Extant plans suggest that it was to be called Prince's Road but it was named Wilbraham Road, perhaps in deference to William Egerton's father, perhaps his son—they were both named Wilbraham.

The new centre of the town quickly established its importance and those interested in social developments could do worse than examine how housing changed in style as time went on and distance from the station increased.[85]

At the opening of the station there were 200 season-ticket holders, five years later there were 600, but there was still a demand for the 'bus service and the cessation in service was brief; soon it was running again and continued to do so until the arrival of the electric tramcar at Lane End (Sandy Lane/High Lane). The two regular drivers were Pug Johnson and Hell Fire Jack.

Horse trams never ran to Chorlton. Their nearest approach was Alexandra Road and Brooks's Bar and when they started to serve that area, the horse 'bus service was cut back to the Prince of Wales.[86] The Manchester Carriage Company was now the Carriage and Tramways Company, having changed its title in 1880 when its sphere of operation was extended.

In 1901, Manchester Corporation took over the operations of the Tramways Company and rapidly the many routes were electrified. On 13th April 1903, a service from Belle Vue via Brooks's Bar and Upper Chorlton Road arrived at West Point —thus penetrating, just, the boundary of the township. On 7th May 1907, the service was extended to Lane End which was to remain the stage for fare calculation for many years.[87] The occasional 'bus service from Flixton and Stretford already noted, was, by 1903, a regular service between Urmston, Stretford and Chorlton stations.[88]

Ever ready to capitalise on assets, the Tramway Department extended the line to Southern Cemetery Gates on 31st May 1911 and when the connection between the Cemetery Gates and West Didsbury was opened on 15th June 1913, it was possible to introduce the 45 and 46 Circular Route services.

The Alexander Road service was extended to Wilbraham Road on 19th February 1913, and then to Egerton Road on 9th May of the same year. This was to be the terminus for five months until the railway bridge was sufficiently strengthened and the final length to join the Barlow Moor Road line was opened on 13th October.[89] This almost completed the Chorlton tramway pattern. Facilities for turning and waiting were provided at the 'Terminus' in 1915, and the Seymour Grove line was built in 1921. Two tiny bits of trackwork, the 'north' connection between Barlow Moor and Wilbraham Roads in 1928 and changes at the terminus completed the picture.

The introduction of electric tramways started the slow decline in the importance of the railway and opened up large new areas for housing development. Probably there is no finer example of this than Chorltonville. This most remarkable example of estate planning, though not the first by fourteen years, set a standard for others to try to emulate. Even today more than sixty years after the birth of the scheme, the estate is one of the most desirable residential areas of Manchester suburbia.

The original scheme as envisaged by Alderman J. H. Dawson, J.P., F.R.S.A.[90] provided an opportunity for those of Hulme and Chorlton on Medlock, who wished, to leave the slums for more congenial surroundings. However, when given the opportunity, not one person was prepared to leave his old home and the whole concept had to be changed. Rents were as low as £24 per annum with rates in addition. A qualification for tenancy was the holding of two £5 shares in Chorltonville Limited, though more could be held (and frequently were since the interest helped to reduce the rent charge). Of the estate's 36 acres, $5\frac{1}{2}$ were used to provide recreational facilities with five tennis courts and a bowling green with a fine pavilion. The children were provided with their own playground and to encourage the cultivation of gardens, a flower show was promoted each year.

The formal opening of the 'New Garden Village' was performed by Mr. Harry Nuttall, M.P. for the Stretford Division, on 7th October 1911. No two adjacent units are of the same design but, apart from the forgivable failure to anticipate the need for garages, the estate carries its age with extremely good grace. Changing conditions have brought to an end the original principle of renting and owner-occupancy is now the rule; the trams which were five minutes and the station twelve minutes away according to the original prospectus, have both gone but the diesel 'bus which carries the destination CHORLTONVILLE has failed to penetrate what remains a secluded monument of one man's foresight.

Transport changes between the two wars resulted in the replacement of the tram by the ubiquitous motor bus. The last Manchester tram ran in 1947, the last day of operation in Chorlton being 26th August 1946. The story of 'bus development and operation is very complex and must be left to a specialist historian to unfold. [91]

FROM VILLAGE TO SUBURB

It took little more than a decade for the impact of the arrival of the railway at Stretford to make itself felt. By 1861 the new householders along Edge Lane were asking the Stretford Gas Company to supply them with gas. In 1862 this form of lighting was installed in the Beech Road Wesleyan Chapel, and in the same year the Manchester Gas Works was instructed to extend its main to Brookbank Bridge to supply Chorlton.

Water had also become a problem. In the past wells and the brook had met the demand, but these supplies were by now both inadequate and contaminated. A requisition to Manchester in 1863 resulted in the laying of a 3 in. main to the Green the following year. As Chortlon grew there were many extensions and a new main was necessary in 1877.

Under the Public Health Act of 1872, the Boards of Guardians were constituted as Rural Sanitary Authorities. There having previously been no sanitary authority for Chorlton, Burnage, Withington or Didsbury townships, the new Rural Sanitary Authority appointed the Guardians representing these townships to a committee to inquire into what precise form the new authority for these places should take. That there was opportunity for manoeuvre indicates the relative laxity in local government at the time, but being unable to get any unanimity of opinion, it was decided to form a single authority to administer the four townships.

The responsibilities in local government assigned to these authorities were much greater than the restrictive title suggests, but when it was discovered that administration was not as convenient as had been expected, the authority, under the provisions of the Public Health Acts of 1848, 1872 and 1875, sought, and was granted, a provisional order constituting the four townships a Local Board District.

It was in 1875, under the Sanitary Authority, that the streets were first gas lit. To be realistic, there were four lamps along the route of the gas main; at West Point, Manchester Road/Barlow Moor Road, St. Clement's Road/High Lane and the Green. This last was sited in what is now the roadway near the present telephone kiosk since the Green was, at the time, still Miss Wilton's private garden. The four standards were very large and ornate which perhaps placated the villagers for the long delay occasioned by the refusal of the farmers to pay the lighting rate to cover the cost.

By its establishment the Local Board achieved as much power as a corporate town! The first election for membership of the Withington Local Board was held on 2nd November 1876 and fifteen members were elected, of whom three represented Chorlton. The new Board was officially constituted on 7th November and their offices in Lapwing Lane, West Didsbury, was built in 1881.

The elections were peculiar in the extreme. One vote was allowed for each £50 of rateable value up to £300 for both owner and occupier so that an owner-occupier could possibly enjoy twelve votes! Ballot papers were distributed three clear days before the day of the election and practically any method of collection seems to have been acceptable—including leaving them at the nearest public house or handing them to the land-lord. The possibilities of irregularity were many.

As has already been suggested, as Manchester grew, Chorlton became a popular haunt of its working class. Its remoteness often cloaked such petty crimes as poaching, illegal gaming and, probably most rife, drinking out of hours, particularly on a Sunday when only bona fide travellers could be served. There was seldom any serious crime and, as policing was administered from Stretford at this time, it was just as well.

The one crime which stirred the nation, and which still causes controversy from time to time, was the assassination of Police Constable Nicholas Cock on 1st August 1876. To put the story in its simplest terms, let us parade the characters. Charles Peace was a petty pilferer, a small-time burglar, lame, fond of playing the fiddle and with a false sense of his attractiveness to the opposite sex. He was clever enough to 'do' jobs away from his home in Sheffield and to 'case' them thoroughly beforehand. The Habron brothers, John and William, were local sons of the soil and not above a little poaching from time to time. Constables Cock and Beanland were under Superintendent Bent of the Lancashire Constabulary at Stretford and this last individual was responsible for much of the enquiry into the affair.

By 1876 Mr. Cunliffe Brooks had developed Jackson's Moss (Whalley Range in deference to his native place), and the new homes of the wealthy and upper middle-class had reached as far as the newly-styled West Point. The most considerable house hereabouts was that of Samuel Gratrix, now, enlarged, the Seymour Hotel but then surrounded by a high brick wall.

There was considerable ill-will between the Habron brothers and the two local constables over poaching of which the brothers were suspected. Some little time prior to the event John was heard to threaten, in the Royal Oak Inn, that they would 'get' Cock so that when that constable was found shot dead against the wall of Mr. Gratrix's house on the night of the 1st August, it was only to be expected that they would be the obvious suspects.

Reading the evidence presented almost a century ago with the cold clinical judgment which comes of hind sight, the case for accusing 18-year old William Habron seems frail, but on it he was found guilty at his trial later in the month.

On 26th December 1876, possibly because of a plea of clemency, possibly because the Home Office had some doubt, the sentence was respited to life imprisonment.

Some two and a half years later Charles Peace was appre-hended for, and found guilty of, another murder. He confessed to being guilty of the murder of P.C. Cock. His confession fitted the events of the night with greater accuracy than did the evi-dence offered against Habron. It was to the effect that he had previously 'viewed' the house in Seymour Grove which he intended to burgle and had travelled to Manchester on this night with that in view. Walking down the road (probably Upper Chorlton Road) he passed two constables (these were Cock and Beanland) and though he believed that the police never bothered with a well-dressed individual, on this occasion one of the constables followed him. Peace was disturbed when he entered the garden by the constable (it would be Cock) and tried to evade him but on being cornered threatened to shoot. The threat had no effect and Cock advanced with his staff as his only weapon. When he tried to hold Peace, the burglar shot with the intention of wounding his arm and so releasing his hold. Instead the bullet entered Cock's chest and Peace was thus able to escape.

P.C. Cock was buried in the old churchyard and the Lancashire Police erected a magnificent marble headstone with helmet,
gloves, bulls-eye lantern and truncheon carved in relief. In
1956, after the closing of the Old Church, the headstone was
taken to the County Police Headquarters at Hutton, near
Preston, where it can be seen set against the main drive. It is
unfortunate that the monumental sculptor made a mistake in the
spelling of 'assassinated'

An old cuttings books of the 1885 period tells of the capture
of an 'Invincible Moonlighter' in Chorlton. This gang, with
such a fanciful name, was of thugs and murderers from Ireland.
They had broken into a house at Ballyhoneys, Co. Mayo,
attempted to murder the householder's wife by gunshots,
assaulted her and then wrecked the furniture. After long investi-
gation the leader, one Patrick Freeley, was traced to Chorlton.
Informants reported him to be working as a farm labourer for
Mr. Bailey, then the tenant of Holly Farm, Beech Road (now
Ivy Farm) and it was to there that two Irish detectives and Sgt.
Joseph Chappell of Stretford, went. Afraid lest Freeley had
received warning of their coming they approached carefully
and, on seeing Mr. Edward Bailey leave the house, they prompt-
ly arrested him and read out the warrant. The error was sorted
out and the officers despatched to Back-end field where Freeley
was arrested with nothing more than 'all right' as acknowledgement. He was taken back to Ireland to stand trial. The newspaper reporter gave an account at great length of the accused's
stay in Chorlton and ended, almost as an anti-climax, 'the
affair has caused quite a sensation in Chorlton'.

In 1885 the Lancashire police authority erected the police
station, with cells, in Beech Road. Surely a sign that Chorlton
was becoming a part of the civilized world! The following year
the Chorlton Penny Bank first offered its services in the Old
School on Saturday evenings, on the first night 102 accounts
were opened.

For some time the villagers, or more likely the new residents
of the township, concerned at the fire risk, had been petitioning
the Local Board to supply fire fighting equipment, so, in 1888,
they were provided with a hand-pump and ladder with a cart
for conveyance. This was kept under the wall which flanked the
Lloyd Platt Hotel.

The Local Board had a life of but eighteen years. It came to its end on 30th December 1894, leaving behind as its memorial the Chorlton sewage works—so much a model of its time that the installation was the only one not closed down as inefficient as Manchester extended its boundaries. Under the provisions of the Local Government Act, elections for the new Withington Urban District Council were held the previous 17th November when Messrs. Burgess, Bingham and Norquoy were elected to represent the Chorlton-cum-Hardy ward. The first named of the three played a major part in the making public of Chorlton Green on 1st June 1895, after it had reverted to Lord Egerton from Miss Wilton's occupation. Lord Egerton also provided the Beech Road Recreation Ground and opened it on 16th May 1896.

The new body took over on 31st December with a life destined to be even shorter than that of its predecessor. The expansion of Manchester and, in particular, the problems and finances of being a dormitory area, led to increasing pressure to have the Urban District incorporated into the City of Manchester.[92]

Royal Assent to the Bill for absorption was given on 15th August 1904 and Chorlton-cum-Hardy, with the other three townships, became a part of the sprawling octopus. The first elections were held 1st November and Messrs. E. Farrar, D. Kemp and J. Turner were elected Chorlton's councillors.

For ten years there was a preferential rating system whereby several local functions were undertaken by the 'Withington Committee' of the City Council. Reminders of this period in the form of street ironware inscribed 'M/c Corp. Withington Highways' (or similar) are still in evidence and, with careful looking, one can still find W.U.D.C., and W.L.B. relics.

Public concern with popular education coincided with Chorlton's population explosion and the growing period of local government. In 1845 the Rev. Birley had been instrumental in the building of the Church School which in 1878 was condemned as inadequate by the Board of Education's inspectors. It was replaced by a new building in 1879. By this time enterprising individuals were cashing in on the new class conscious population and private schools were in increasing evidence. Mr. Robert Davies opened the Chorlton Commercial Schools in 1872 in the building which was later to be St. Augustine's church and presbytery. He changed its title to Chorlton High Schools in 1874 and the press of the time spoke highly of the school's successes. There were many schools for young children and young ladies,[93] usually under the guidance of unmarried young women though by 1891 Harold W. Urquart had a grammar school in Beech Road. C. C. Dadley, M.A., opened the Chorlton Grammar School in the house on High Lane opposite York Road in 1896 which lasted until 1930 with Dadley living there until 1936. In 1896 Edward Mostyn opened an art school in the building on High Lane opposite St. John's church, now the Road Union headquarters. Of this building more anon.

The parish's troubles with the siting of the new church and the graveyard were accompanied by troubles associated with the building of the 1879 'National Schools'. There was a local body that felt that a School Board for the district was necessary and the new school should be built as a board school. The Church Party refused to agree to the establishment of broad-based multi-denominational control and so the new school remained under the control of the Established Church.

The Roman Catholic congregation acquired the premises of the old Chorlton High Schools and in 1898 were building a new denominational school, and a new C. of E. school in St. Clement's Road was built in 1901. This building, adjacent to the New Church, was designed to be extended upwards but it was not to be so until 1970, long after the school on the Green had been closed.

An urgent job to be undertaken by Manchester was an extension in school facilities; whether it was already planned by the Urban District or by Manchester in anticipation, a fortnight after Manchester took control, the art school of Tom Mostyn was taken over and opened as a mixed municipal school on 29th August 1904.[95] It provided places for 220 pupils.

Two years later (1st July 1906) a temporary school was opened in Oswald Road and two years later again (17th July 1908) the foundation stone of the permanent Oswald Road School was laid, to be opened 26th April 1909, from which time the High Lane school was closed. From then the story of education in Chorlton is merely a matter of dates.

The extensions in education were paralleled by other public services. Chorlton's telephone exchange opened in 1895 with

J. Grimes and C. H. Watson as the first subscribers; by 1909 there were 290. Electricity from the Corporation undertaking was available, with Ebor House and Chorlton Pharmacy (Kemps) as the first users, on 18th December 1902. The gas undertaking took over the supplying of those customers who had previously been supplied by Stretford in March 1906. In 1908 (23rd November) the house on the left-hand corner of Vincent Avenue was opened as a public free library until the present building, on the site of the Red Gate Farm, was opened in November 1914. Perhaps aware that Chorlton was fast losing its rural charm the city started a tree-planting scheme in Manchester Road in 1908.

Being now provided with nearly all the trappings of an up-to-date community, the township's development lay largely in building more and more houses on a rapidly diminishing area of available land. Public baths, long promised, and a park, both in 1928, found the thirties with only Barlow Moor as the sizeable building area left. The generous building density meant that by the outbreak of the second world war the whole was on the point of bursting at the seams. Since 1945 building has had to be confined to the full utilisation of such areas as had previously been too small to warrant consideration; now the much publicised 'Green Belt' of the Mersey floodplain is being whittled away by road construction, and building development is restricted to cleared sites or land which has been sufficiently raised by tipping.

THE CHURCHES

A hundred and twenty years ago there were but two religious factions in Chorlton; it was only to be expected that in the increasing population there would be representatives of many new sects, but, we must start from where we left off.

In 1860, shortly after the arrival of the Rev. William Birley in the parish, it was felt that the growth of the village made increased church accommodation necessary. The Parish Church was in poor condition, especially the roof (possibly as a result of building on the side aisles in 1837) and perhaps this persuaded the rector that a new church was necessary. Lord Egerton was approached and offered a piece of the Pingot Hey at the corner of St. Clement's Road and Edge Lane for a church and churchyard, with a subscription of £500, on the understanding that the endowment was transferred from the Old Church. The proposal for a new church was generally approved, but the suggested site did not meet with the approval of a considerable body of the parishioners who, led by Mr. William Cunliffe Brooks and Mr. Samuel Mendel (of Manley Hall), thought that it should be built on the site of the existing church or nearby in the Back Lane (Hawthorn Road = Ivygreen Road).

The arguments on both sides became heated and bitter. Mr. Brooks and Mr. Mendel, with others, withdrew their promised subscriptions and the Old Church was renovated at Mr. Brooks' expense. This gentleman always showed great interest in the old building and was the donor of the lych-gate as a Jubilee gift in 1888.

In spite of everything, not least the lack of sufficient funds, and without the clear-cut approval of the parish, the building of the new church went ahead until the want of money brought work to a stop and the empty shell remained until 1865. On 8th March of that year, a parish meeting considered the problem of completion and the transfer of the endowment, and by Ellwood's description (and he may well have been there) it could hardly be said to have reflected any credit on those principally concerned. The outcome of the acrimonious meeting, first by show of hands and then by ballot, was that the endowment should be transferred. For some unknown reason the decision was never implemented and the Old Church was to remain the parish church until its closure in February 1940 as a result of frost damage.

The meeting did have the effect of forcing the completion of the nave and chancel. The opening service was on Saturday, 23rd June 1866, but the building was only licensed for divine service; there was to be a thirty-year wait for the consecration. In the meantime the building was slowly completed, the north transept and choir vestry in 1883 and the south transept in 1896.[96] Until consecration, when the land was transferred to the Ecclesiastical Commissioners, the parish paid a yearly rent of 10s. to his Lordship.

As if their troubles with the new church were not enough, there was a separate problem with the graveyard. An anonymous informant caused Dr. Holland, one of Her Majesty's Inspectors of Churchyards to visit Chorlton on 25th November 1869, to enquire into the state of the burial ground. It was the inspector's opinion that there was little or no ground available for new graves and that, therefore, a new burial-ground was necessary. The rector offered the yard of the new church but strong objections were raised by the owners and occupiers of nearby property.

In spite of the report, it seems that things went on very much as before for a further twelve years. Then the Ratepayers' Association drew the attention of the Local Board and the Home Office to the objectionable condition of the yard. Dr. Hoffman held an enquiry in the large room of the Lloyd-Platt Hotel on 25th November 1881 (a coincidence of dates) at which a large gathering of interested parties was present. The Inspector did not need to call all the evidence, he was soon convinced that all was far from well. On 1st February 1882 the churchwardens were notified by the Home Office that, with certain very special exceptions, no further internments would be permitted without their authority.[97]

The Withington Local Board tried to persuade Manchester to allow the same reduced burial charges in the newly opened Southern Cemetery, within the Local Board's area, as was enjoyed by the citizens of Manchester. It was quickly pointed out that the people of the city were in effect subsidising the cemetery from the rate-fund.[98]

While the Church Party were resolving their problems, the Wesleyans were also finding that their chapel in Beech Road was insufficient for their needs. In 1871 approval was forthcoming for a new chapel. A plot of land in Manchester Road was obtained from Lord Egerton at a chief-rent of 2d. per yard and the building was commenced in 1822, being opened on 2nd July 1873. The old organ from Beech Road was transferred to the new building and served there until replaced by a new one in 1876.

A serious fire partially destroyed the chapel on 21st November 1883, the new organ being one casualty. Insurance covered the major part of the cost of restoration and during 1884–85 a Sunday school building was erected at the rear of the restored church.

By 1879 there were sufficient people who followed the Congregational persuasion to encourage the Rev. James A. Macfadyen to seek permission from the Masonic authorities to hold services in the Masonic Hall in High Lane on Sundays.[99] Consent was given but until 1882 they would not countenance the holding of a Sunday school. The first service, Mr. Macfadyen officiating, was held 29th September 1879. On 14th April 1883, Mr. J. C. Needham laid the foundation stone of a school-church and the building was brought into use on 29th September of the same year. There was no waste of time in those days.

The Congregational Church was formally constituted on 3rd December 1884. Mr. Macfadyen died in 1889 and his widow laid the corner stone of the Macfayden Memorial Church on 16th September 1893, The new building was opened for public worship on 25th October 1894.

Way back in 1835 the Rev. John Morton had purchased a plot of land and built thereon a house which he called 'Oakley'. When he died in 1842 the property was bought by Chas. Clarke, J.P., who altered and enlarged it and later sold it to Mr. J. C. Needham. In 1890 Bishop Vaughan founded the Catholid parish of St. Augustine's in Chorlton and Mr. Needham's old house became the 'Priory' (from which Priory Avenue takes its name). A group of Benedictine priests from Fort Augustus in Scotland, led by Father Jerome Vaughan (brother of the Bishop) started their ministrations.

In 1900 the Benedictines left and Father Frederick Holt was appointed Parish Priest. His church was the building in High Lane which had lately been a part of Mr. Davies's Chorlton High Schools and the presbytery was the house adjacent. Two years previously the Rev. John Bilsborrow had laid the foundation stone of a school at the rear so that a neat tidy parochial unit was formed.

In 1916 Father Holt was appointed chaplain to the Withington Hospital and his duties in Chorlton were taken over by Monsignor Joseph Kelly under whose energetic direction work progressed steadily towards the provision of a new and more fitting church. This was opened in June 1927[100] and the occasion was marked by a change of parochial title to St. John's to avoid confusion with St. Augustine's, Chorlton on Medlock.

Monsignor Kelly died in 1930, his successor, Canon Edward McGuinness, M.C., died in 1946 and the present Parish Priest is Father W. J. Sewell.

The phenomenal increase in population, particularly as a result of building in the Wilbraham Road/Egerton Road area of the township, created a demand for a new Church of England parish; so it was that the parish of St. Werburgh's was carved out of the several adjoining parishes, including St. Clement's, in 1898. The foundation stone was laid on the 5th November of the following year and the chancel and transepts were dedicatep in 1900. The church was completed and opened 1st June 1902, and consecrated on 15th July.

Church developments were not yet at an end. The Unitarians opened their church in Wilbraham Road on 9th February 1901; the Macpherson Memorial Primitive Methodist church in High Lane was opened on 20th September 1902 and the Chorlton-cum-Hardy Presbyterian Church of England was established 8th November 1903. There was then a brief pause before the unsatisfied demand made it self felt again, then the foundation stone of the McLaren Memorial Baptist Church on Wilbraham Road was laid on 7th July 1906 and the church opened 29th May 1907, with the Presbyterians laying their foundation stone 1st September of the same year, to be opened on 15th March of the year following.

In Oswald Road in 1909 was opened the Emmanuel Free Church. This was the least successful of them all and though their corrugated iron building was not demolished until February 1972, it had been derelict for many years and before that was used for a long time as the works of a firm of cleaners.

By the first world war the religious expansion had largely exhausted itself. Between the wars the various denominations were generally concerned in maintaining their position and since the second war there has been considerable retrenchment of all sects. The Old Parish Church was demolished in 1949 and replaced, in a sort of way, by the new church of St. Barnabas on Hardy Lane in 1951. The Primitive Methodist church in High Lane was a post-war victim of dwindling congregations, but there is satisfaction to be gained from the recent establishment of several new denominations.

PUBS, POST OFFICES and PALACES

Reference has already been made to the early public houses in Chorlton. The Bowling Green, probably the oldest with a reputed licensing date of 1693 was, as late as the early XIX century, as much a farmhouse as a place of refreshment. The present building is dated 1908, the previous one (of which excellent photographs exist) seems to have been built about 1780. One of its assets was the old village fishpond which was let to 'gentlemen' for their sport but was filled up when Lord Egerton caused to have built a sewer which emptied into Chorlton Brook about 100 yards downstream from Brook Road Bridge. Two early benevolent societies, the 'Old Men's Club' and the 'Old Women's Club' held their weekly meetings at the Bowling Green and instead of paying a rent for the use of a room, each member was charged 3*d*. per week 'drink money'. As many members did not drink and others did not attend in person, this practice caused a great deal of resentment. Otherwise the clubs with a weekly sickness grant of 8*s*. and death benefit of £8 in exchange for a quarterly contribution of 2*s*. 6*d*. was of great benefit and very good value.[101]

The Horse & Jockey, while a very old building (reputed 1520) is not old as a licensed house, dating, so far as can be ascertained, from the beginning of the XIX century. It is essentially a brick building (as early photographs show) and its present Olde Worlde Look dates from quite late in this century. Those who think of brewery take-overs as a modern phenomenon might reflect that when the house was sold to a brewery at the turn of the century, it brought £10,000.

The reason for the name 'Horse & Jockey' has been ascribed to the use of the house by those attending the races on the Scaffold Field. There is no evidence of this, their contemporary existence must have been short and, by Ellwood's records, there was a small public house (of which nothing more is known) on Nell Lane, not far from where the Southern Hotel now is.

The Bridge Inn was the Greyhound for a long time after the bridge was built, but it is still more usually referred to as 'Jackson's Boat'. Its important associations have already been told. It is an interesting point that if one goes from the bridge to Stretford by the most direct motor route, three successive houses bear the name of 'The Bridge Inn'.

Established, apparently, later than 1872 there was on Beech Road an ale house kept by a man named James Wilkinson. In 1883 he was summoned, with a cab driver, Robert Duffy, for supplying drink on a Sunday out of hours. Duffy said that he had come from All Saints whereas he had only come from Canning Street—a few yards short of the requisite three miles. The origin of the name of Trevor Arms has defied search. So far only one other of this name, at Marford, near Wrexham, is known. The Trevor is still there but the Traveller's Rest, almost opposite, and known earlier as the Traveller's Call, and earlier still as the Robin Hood, licenced 1832, has gone. Left behind is a single relic in a fragment of the gents' toilet in the yard behind the confectioners.

At Lane End we have already mentioned, in connection with badger-baiting, the Black Horse. This house was granted its licence in 1832 but had it revoked about 1870 for persistent offences against Sunday opening regulations. Another small house was the Royal Oak at Martledge, the present hotel stands on the same site, which was popular with farm labourers (we have already referred to the Habron brothers in this connection). The remaining house, the Lloyd Platt, usually known as 'The Lloyds' was built about 1870 by James Platt on land belonging to George Lloyd. The name suggests that this was a business partnership.

Of other licensed houses in or near, only the Seymour is of interest in view of its origin.

This is perhaps the most convenient point to mention the other notable place of refreshment in the annals of Chorlton—the Pop Cottage which stood on Manchester Road until the construction of the railway bridge in 1879 made its demolition necessary. It was kept by the Hesketh family and Betty Bates (*nee* Hesketh) was one of the characters of the village. It carried the legend:

> Prime Pop and Nettle Beer,
> always ripe and ready here.
> If all the pop was like mine,
> it would be drunk instead of wine.

In very early days Chorlton's mail was left or collected at the Bull's head on Chester Road in Hulme and farmers on their way to or from Manchester usually undertook this service. Later a post office was established in Stretford and served a large surrounding area. The Stretford Post master was Henry Moore, who also performed the duty of postman. His average daily delivery was about fifty packets, of which Chorlton would on average be represented by half-a-dozen, but he also collected the mail on his way.

His round covered Old Trafford, West Point, Chorlton, Barlow Hall, Jackson's Boat, Sale, Ashton on Mersey, Carrington, Woodsend, Davyhulme, Dumplington, Urmston and back to Stretford. This distance of about twenty-six miles he covered on foot between 5 a.m. and noon, and on occasions he would swim the flooded meadows across to Sale rather than go round. With his father he carried on a business of glaziers and plumbers, and as the only such between Didsbury and Eccles, he would be seen setting off with his glass frame on his back soon after dinner. One wonders how he found time also to be the agent for the Yorkshire Fire & Life Insurance Company.

After the postal reforms of Rowland Hill in 1840, the increase in business made it necessary to open many more offices and Chorlton's first was opened on 1st January 1857, in connection with a stationers shop, kept by Thomas Taylor, on the corner of the Acre and Beech Road. By 1890 the growth of the New Village had made a compromise necessary and Edwin Foden was combining a chemists' business with a post office on High Lane in the shop which is now a cycle dealers. It is within the memory of the not-so-old that the steps by which the Stretford mail carrier mounted and dismounted his horse still existed there.

The year 1894 found Mr. Foden, his chemists and the post office in premises on Barlow Moor Road now occupied by the Trustees Savings Bank. On 20th January 1901, the business of this office was transferred to a new building which was to remain in use until it was blitzed in December 1940. The site was later used for the Fleming Hall and is now the Lipton supermarket. But to return to the turn of the century, it was recognized that Chorlton had acquired two centres of population by re-opening an office in the Market Place in 1900, in a position which still houses the Beech Road sub-office.

With the blitz of 1940 the main office moved to premises on the corner of Manchester Road and Keppel Road, vacated by the M.E.T.A. Manufacturing Co., and there it remained until the present building, next door to the old site, was opened 11th December 1961.

Throughout the years, until the advent of canned entertainment, the village made its own amusement and of the early pastimes we have already spoken. Probably as a logical extension of the mummers and morris dancers tradition a brass band was formed in 1820—John Axon was the drummer and his brother James made the drum; when it was finished it was too big to go through the door. In 1867 was established the 'Penny Readings' which proved to be very popular with people to whom was thus revealed a world that in their illiterate state would otherwise be closed.

But in a world where the wonders of entertainment were yet to be invented, the New Chorltonians introduced a whole range of cultural and educational societies. It is probably true that the old Chorltonians largely ignored these innovations but there was sufficient money and support available without their help. A Reading Room was opened in 1874, ten years later the Literary Association was formed, and after that they came fast and furious. By 1910 there were 36 organisations including seven tennis clubs, two bowling clubs, three lacrosse clubs and no less than nine football clubs. Some fell by the wayside and some changed their scope as, for instance, the Horticultural Society which (heedless to the warning spelt out by the 'Great South to North Procession of Motor Cars' which passed through the township in 1900) changed its title in 1903 to the Horticultural and Horse Society.

The Great War of 1914 put an end to this type of community activity for after 1918 it was never to be the same again. The shape of things to come, for those with the foresight to recognise it, had been the establishment, in the first decade of the present century, of the Chorlton Pavilion. This was on Wilbraham Road, between the station and Buckingham Road—today the site of a petrol station—and amongst a variety of entertainment it presented the bioscope (or moving pictures) to a bewildered audience. In 1909 it was bought by H. D. Moorhouse, a Manchester solicitor, and was the first house of what was to become the extensive local HDM circuit of the between-the-wars period. Between 1911 and 1915 it was known as the Chorlton Pavilion and Winter Gardens and was still in existence after the first war.

The Palais de Luxe Cinema, now the Tesco Supermarket, was opened in 1915 and retained its name through to its closing

Hough End Hall from Booker's History of Didsbury and Chorlton Chapels.

Nell Lane looking from the Chorlton Brook bridge. (source unknown).

Chorltonville, sports pavilion and backs of houses in Meadow Bank. c. 1912. (pub. W. A. Cooper, stationer, 30 Barlow Moor Road).

Hough End Hall, c. 1935, from Nell Lane. (photo. author).

Old cottages in Sandy Lane, c. 1935 (photo. author).

Jackson's boat bridge and the Bridge Inn, c. 1895. (photo. the late C. E. Jones).

West front of Barlow Hall, c. 1895. (photo. the late C. E. Jones).

*The inner court of Barlow Hall, c. 1890, but little changed to-day.
(photo. the late C. E. Jones).*

about 1958. Not so the Majestic which, in spite of carrying that name on its facade was the Savoy from its opening, then the A.B.C., and lastly the Gaumont before its closure and ultimate conversion into an undertakers' establishment. The last cinema was the Rivoli opened 1937 and closed during and after the war as a result of enemy action. Under the names of the Essoldo and now the Classic, it remains as the only local cinema in business.

In the late twenties and early thirties, the age of Picture Palaces and Super Dance Halls, was built the Chorlton Palais de Dance, still with us in the guise of a club. Before and after the first war there were occasional visits of a circus or fun fair to the village tip at the end of Hawthorn Road (= Ivygreen Road) but in the end the property builders moved in and appropriated the site for housing.

The hall of the Conservative Club (The Public Hall) once provided facilities for dramatic society presentations, society dances and other public functions but economic necessity has withdrawn this facility and Chorlton is now ill-provided with suitable premises. How far this is responsible for the dearth of the old style of communal activity cannot be assessed, but it is painfully obvious that Chorlton in the evening is dead. The occasional couple wander towards the public house or the Classic, the 'bus to Stretford experiences a rush as the bingo players take themselves away and the kids hang around the street corners and finally, from boredom, find some mischief to do. About eleven o'clock those who have been out shuffle back and a few more ghostly blue shadows flick across the curtains to join the many more that have been flickering all night. In sixty years from the bioscope at the Pavilion to the television in the sitting-room!

THE EGERTONS

The Withington estates of the Mosleys and the Barlow estate were acquired through purchase by the Egerton family. Through family connections and further purchases they eventually owned a considerable area of Chorlton so that the building boom found them in an excellent position to benefit. Though the family has had a considerable influence on the development of the township, details of it are relatively unknown. It is hoped that the following brief notes will correct this.

It was Samuel Egerton who bought the Manor of Withington on the break-up of the Mosley connections with this area, and with this he purchased other large land holdings. On Samuel's death in 1780 his property passed to his sister Hester who was married to William Tatton of Wythenshawe Hall.

The Lordship of the Manor, which at one time had been held by Lady Ann Bland, thus had a second Lady of the Manor, albeit for a very short period for she died in the same year as her brother. She changed her surname back to her maiden name (probably to conform to a requirement in the will) and on her death the property passed to her son, William Egerton. It was William who commenced the building of the present Tatton Hall but it was still incomplete on his death in 1806. In 1785 William Egerton purchased the Barlow estate. The first tenant of Barlow Hall was Thomas Walker, boroughreeve of Manchester in 1790, great political reformer and a Jacobite. His son, born at Barlow Hall but later of Longford Hall, was a practical philanthropist and author of 'The Original'.

Wilbraham Egerton, son of William, died in 1856; his son, William Tatton Egerton, was a Member of Parliament for Cheshire and died in 1883, having been created Baron Egerton of Tatton in 1859. His son, another Wilbraham, was created Earl Egerton and Viscount Salford in the Diamond Jubilee year 1897. As chairman of the Manchester Ship Canal Company he cut the first sod of that undertaking in 1887 and as the owner of so much land in this area he influenced the general direction of building development by clauses written into title deeds. At the same time he protected himself by instituting a chief rent on the land which was sold.

On his death in 1909 the earldom became extinct as he had no son. His younger brother Alan de Tatton Egerton became Baron Egerton and on his death, his son, Maurice Egerton, became the fourth Baron. He was destined to be the last of the line. He was unmarried—indeed he appears to have been very much a woman hater and when he died in 1958 there was nobody to follow on.

Tatton Hall is now administered on behalf of the National Trust by the Cheshire County Council. Most of the properties have been sold though the Manor of Withington remains in being, with the executors of the estate being technically the Lord of the Manor.

And so the story of Chorlton and Hardy, of Martledge and Barlow, and of their surroundings must come to an end. In concluding his 1886 series, Ellwood said:

'His task in the collection of the many details . . . has been laborious, but pleasurable, and he trusts that his readers have not been without pleasure in their perusal.'

The present author can but echo the same sentiment, having additionally found it very challenging. In another half-century another chronicler will be able to blend today's story into the ever-unfolding record of events, but now it remains to thank my mother for having endured the almost endless clacking of the typewriter, to Mrs. E. Baxendale for having courageously volunteered to check the script, and to the Morten brothers, David and Eric, for being so patient, and bid my readers God-speed.

NOTE

[83] The service in 1879 had been: Horse & Jockey dep. 8 a.m., 8-30, 10, 12-noon, 2 p.m., 5, 6, 7 and 8 on week-days and 3 p.m., 4, 5, 6, 7, 8 and 9 on Sundays.

[84] This road, which otherwise cuts an almost straight course bent in order to join Edge Lane at the same point as did Cow Lane (which ran through to the brick-croft, the end is now Hampton Road).

[85] Corkland Road (was Cavendish Road) and the roads off it show the changes very well.

[86] In 1896: from the Green every 30 min., 10 a.m. to 1 p.m. then every 15 mins. to 10 p.m. Sundays every 15 min. 11 a.m. to 10 p.m.
In 1898: from the Green every 15 min., 10 a.m. (Sundays 11 a.m.) to 10.15 p.m.
In 1902: from the Green every 30 min., 9.30 a.m. (11 a.m. Sunday) to 10 p.m.
In 1907: from the Green every 30 min., 8-30 a.m. to 10-30 p.m., (Sundays 10 a.m. to 10 p.m.).

[87] In 1920 the service was: Chorlton to Hightown, via All Saints and Exchange, 5 a.m. and every 30 min. to 7 a.m., then 7-28 a.m. and every 5 min. to 11-13 p.m., afterwards until 12-03 a.m. to Princess Road. Sundays at 8-20 a.m., 9, 9-30 then every 5 min. to 1 p.m., then 1-12 and every 5 min. to 10-42 p.m. (to Exchange) and 11-32 to Princess Road. The last car to Chorlton left Exchange at 11-25 p.m. on weekdays and 10-46 p.m. on Sundays.
In 1913 one could travel for 1d.: Alexandra Road or the Prince of Wales to High Lane; Seymour Grove or Alexandra Road South/Wilbraham Road to Southern Cemetery Gates or High Lane to West Didsbury.

[88] Every 30 min. 12-30 to 11-45 p.m. On Sundays every hour 2 to 10-10 p.m. This was probably the lineal forerunner of the old North-Western 22X route which used to terminate at Chorlton Station.

[89] The tracks were extended along Wilbraham Road to Fallowfield, 8th December 1924.

[90]   Father of Mr. H. Frank Dawson, the Estate Agent. The agents for Chorlton-ville Ltd. were Dawson and Vowles Ltd., of Wilbraham Road.

[91]   Publications of the Manchester Transport Museum Society are satisfying this need.

[92]   Fletcher Moss in Fifty Years of Public Work in Didsbury gives an excellent account of local politics at this period.

[93]   Ellwood, S. M. G., Ch. XXIV.

[94]   Ellwood, S. M. G., Ch. XIII.

[95]   Similarly Manchester took over the private Whalley Range High School for Girls in Withington Road in August 1908.

[96]   Ellwood, S. M. G., Ch. IX.

[97]   Ellwood, S. M. G., Ch. XII.

[98]   Southern Cemetery was consecrated by Bishop Fraser 26th September 1879, formally 9th October by C. Grundy, Mayor of Manchester. First internment 14th October. The Crematorium, the second in the country (the first was in Worthing) was opened 22nd August 1892, by the Duke of Westminster.

[99]   Now the Irish Club.

[100] The Presbytery was the home of Sir Thomas Seymour Mead of provision-shop fame.

[101] Ellwood, S. M. G., Ch. XXV.

APPENDIX I

Curates and Rectors

SC—Stipendiary Curate * Assistant Clergy

1598	'A reader who keepeth a school'
1604	Roger Worthington 'lector or Reader'
1617	John Dickenson 'Reader and Schoolmaster'
(1636)–1639	Rev. John Bradshaw (tr. to Didsbury)
1639 –1647	Rev. John Pollett (dispossessed)
1647 –1651	Rev. Richard Benson (died in office)
1651 –1654	Rev. John Adcroft (or Odcroft)
1654 –1655	James Jackson (unordained)
1655 – ?	Rev. James Jackson (ordained 5.VI.'55)
(c) 1673	(Edward ?) Richardson
? –1691	Joshua Hyde (unordained or Deacons' Orders)
1716 –1717	Rev. John Thomas
1717 – ?	Rev. Joseph Dale (also of Birch)
1720 – ?	(Rev. Thomas Wright ? (from Didsbury?) (also of Birch?))
1754?—1766	Rev. Robert Oldfield
?	(Thomas Beeley ? (S.C.?))
1766 –1771	Rev. Thomas Assheton
1771 –1789	Rev. John Salter (died in office)
	1782–1789 Joshua Brookes (S.C.)
1789 –1791	Rev. Joshua Brookes
1791 –1805	Rev. N. Mosley Cheek (died in office)
	1796– ? Rev. Roger Mashiter (S.C.)
	1801–1807 Rev. Samuel Stephenson (S.C.)
1805 –1816	Rev. George Hutchinson
	1807–1812 George Holt ('a literate man')
	1812 ? Rev. John Collins (S.C.)
1816 –1833	Rev. R. H. Whitelock (also Vicar of Skillington, curate of St. Mark's, Cheetham, and Postmaster of Manchester)
1833 –1836	Rev. Peter Hordern (died in office)
1836 –1843	Rev. John Morton (died in office)
1843 –1859	Rev. William Birley
1859 –1892	Rev. J. E. Booth

1892 –1911 Rev. F. E. Thomas
           1900–1904   Rev. T. E. Floyd*
           1904–1910   Rev. C. R. Thomas*
           1909–1911   Rev. F. W. Norburn*

1911 –1915 Rev. J. S. Bateson
           1911–1914   Rev. R. J. Blain*
           1912–1915   Rev. W. H. T. Russell*
           1914–1916   Rev. S. L. Caiger*

1915 –1928 Rev. J. H. T. Renshaw
           1915–1918   Rev. J. A. Duff*
           1918   Rev. R. Argyle*
           1919–1922   Rev. E. B. Clarke*
           1922–1926   Rev. F. Knattries*

1928 –1932 Rev. W. Preston
           1928–1929   Rev. B. Edwards*
           1929–1932   Rev. H. D. Gledsdale*

1932 –1948 Rev. G. A. Deakin
           1932–1935   Rev. K. Mitchell*
           1935–1937   Rev. J. Heywood*
           1935–1938   Rev. W. Garlick*
           1937–1940   Rev. R. S. Jones*
           1939–1942   Rev. C. M. Cameron*
           1943–1948   Rev. N. Wallworth*

1948 –1952 Rev. Ross Hook
           1949–1953   Rev. L. S. Rivett*
           1951–1954   Rev. J. T. Annett*

1952 –1967 Rev. D. Ratledge
           1954–1956   Rev. B. P. Brownless*
           1958–1960   Rev. A. C. Grice*
           1959–1962   Rev. R. R. Carmyllie*
           1962–1965   Rev. M. J. Peel*
           1965–1968   Rev. C. G. W. Pilkington*

1968 – Rev. D. Bonser
           1968–1971   Rev. J. Pullen*
           1971–   Rev. D. T. Thomas*

APPENDIX II

Bibliography

Family Memoirs. Sir Oswald Mosley 1849. Printed for private circulation.

S.M.G.   South Manchester Gazette. Articles by Thos. L. Ellwood. 1885.

H.C.D.C.   A History of the Ancient Chapels of Didsbury and Chorlton. Rev. John Booker. 1857.

Wesleyan Church Handbook. Thos. L. Ellwood. 1895.

H.S.C.   History of Stretford Chapel. H. T. Crofton, 3 vols. 1899, 1901, 1903.

H.D.   A History of Didsbury. Ivor R. Million. 1969.

Blessed Ambrose Barlow. Dom. Julian Stoner, O.S.B., n.d.

Books of the Pilgrimages to Old Homes. Fletcher Moss, 7 vols, various dates. References to the Barlow Family.

Old Chorlton. Published by Sarll's Electric Press (c) 1905. Text either by Ellwood or a 'pinch' of his writings.

Concise Oxford Dictionary of English Place Names.

H.W.   A History of Withington. Kenneth Whittaker. 1959 (reprint 1967).

St. Clement's Parish Magazine. Various issues.

Manchester City News. Various issues.

Old Stretford. J. E. Bailey, F.S.A. 1878.

Old Stretford. Sir Bosdin T. Leech. 1910.

History of Birch Chapel. Rev. John Booker. 1854.

History of Local Government in Manchester. Arthur Redford. 3 vols. 1939.

Rich Inheritance. N. J. Frangopulo. 1962.

Memorials of St. Ann's Church. Chas. Wareing Bardsley. 1877.

Ampleforth Journal, Autumn 1970, Vol. LXXV, pt. III, pps. 392–394. (Father Ambrose)

King of the Lags. David Ward 1963 (Charles Peace)

Did Peace commit the Whalley Range Murder.? anon. 1879.

Folk-lore old customs and tales of my neighbours. by Fletcher Moss. 1898.

Ballads and Songs of Lancashire. John Harland. 1865.

The Bridgewater Canal. Bi-centenary Handbook. 1961.

History of Manchester Railways. anon. 1882 (act. William Harrison).

Chronological List of the Railways of Lancashire 1828–1939. M. D. Greville. 1953.

Chorltonville. Descriptive brochure. 'Chorltonville Limited' 1911.

Barlow Family Records. Rt. Hon. Sir Montague Barlow. 1932.

APPENDIX III

The Protestation of 1641
The following persons took the oath:

CHOLLERTON

John Pollett
James Hopwood
James Williamson
William Jackson
James Williamson
James Baguley
John Hughes
John Hodgkinson
Willia. Barlow
Raphe Hulme
Ralph Shelmerdine
George Hulme
John Gimney
Oliver Giddall
John Warburton
John Hunte
Joseph Gee
Samell Hardy
John Hardy

Nicholas Waynewright
Richard Jackson
James Williamson
James Birche
Alexander Hartcliffe
Randle Warburton
Lawrence Typpings
Nathaniel Gee
Henrie Litherland
Willia. Hartley
Alexandra Chorlton
Hugh Gimney
Roberte Sutton
John Wood
Edward Greenhong
Edward Coppock
Lawrence Crowther
Ralph Hunt

Ja. Jollie
John Williamson
William Harison
James Barlowe
William Grantham
Richard Sharrack
John Benson
Steven Edwards
James Hartley
Thomas Robinson
Robert Higham
George Brooke
Ralph Baylie
James Hartley
John Waynewright
Jonathan Gee
Thomas Blomeley
Willia. Baguley

MANSLEACHE

John Fletcher
Randle Hollinworth
Robert Highfield
als Mason
Raphe Daniell
William Rainshawe

William Hollinworth
Alexander Wyshawe
Henrie Mason the
younger
William Arstall
Addam Hoaldeng

Nathaniel Taylor
Thomas Shelmer-
dine

John Didsburie

HARDIE

Thomas Hulme
Thomas Blomeley
Richard Hulme

Robert Hartley
John Parkinson
George Jackson

James Parkinson
Alexander Smith
John Hulme

Thomas Smith Alexander Barlowe* James Chorlton
John Barlow George Townley Nicholas Hartley
Robert Blemeley eles
Kinges

* The lord of Barlow at this time was Alexander. In view of the absence of dissenting names it poses an interesting query.

APPENDIX IV

Returns of Population, etc.

1341   Tithe of one ninth on corn, wool and lambs had a cash value of 10s. per annum.

1599   Tithe rents produced 11s. 1d.

1642   Population of those over 18 yrs. was 84. In Chorlton 55, in Martledge 13 and in Hardy 16.

1692   Assessment for Land Tax £236. 15s.

1714   Population 325; 65 families.

1774   Population 378; 78 families.

1801   Population 513.

1811   Population 619; 112 families, 310 males, 309 females, 109 houses.

1815   Assessment for County Rate £2,941.

1821   Population 624.

1829   Assessment for County Rate £4,314.

1831   Population 668.

1841   Population 632. Assessment for County Rate £4,579.

1851   Population 761; 384 males, 377 females, 146 houses.

1853   Assessment for County Rate £4,241.

1861   Population 739; 360 males, 379 females, 147 houses.

1871   Population 1,653; 765 males, 888 females, 242 houses.

1876   Rateable value £92,000.

1881   Population 2,332; 1,049 males, 1,283 females, 454 houses. Rateable value £120,000.

1891   Population 4,741; 2,088 males, 2,653 females, 944 houses.

1895   Population (estimated) 5,600.

1901   Population 9,026.

1909   Population (estimated) 15,353. 3,060 houses.

1911   Population 24,977*.

The rapidly increasing excess of females over males after 1851 reflects the influx of families who employed maids, cooks and other young women 'in service'.

* After the turn of the century, changes in local government boundaries prevented population figures being strictly comparable.

APPENDIX V

The Margaret Usherwood Charity

In the aisle of the Old Parish Church lies the following inscribed stone:

Here
lieth the Earthly remains
of Margaret Uſherwood of
Chorlton who departed this
life the 19th of November 1748
who through her benevolence
and Charity left to the Families
of Warburtons & Williamſons
Reſiding in Chorlton the uſe
of Sixty five Pounds in order
to bring up Six of their Children
to School under certain
Reſtrictions which if Fulfilled
Otherwise to Six other Poor
Children in Chorlton For
which her Truſtees Have
Erected this Stone.

Jonathan			Lowe
Samuel	}	Truſtees	Parkinſon
Richard			Jones
James (?)			Knight

Ref. Booker, H.C.D.C. p. 316/7

APPENDIX VI

Forms of Spelling recorded by Booker and Ellwood

These are given for interest only. The variety of spellings has no significance, they were written as spoken.

Chorlton	Charlton	Charleton	Cherlton
Cherleton	Chorleton	Chowlerton	Chowrton
Chowerton	Chowreton	Chollerton	Chorllerton
Martledge	Marsleach	Mansleache	Meloche
Melsthelache	Mollsfrellach	Menshallach	Melshelache
Moschellache	Melshawlache	Melschelache	Melsthellache
Melstholache	Molsfrelache	Mersey Lache	
Hardy	Hardie		

INDEX

Old Hall Farm, 25, 63
Omnibus services, early, 89, 90, 92

Park Eye, 4
Parkinson, James, 56
Pavilion & Winter Gardens, 108
Peace, Charles, 95
Peacock Farm, 39
Penance, 82
Plague, 18
Pollett, Rev. John, 54
Pop Cottage, 106
Presbyterian Church of England, 104
Prestwich, family, 35
Primitive Methodist Chapel, 104
Prize fighting, 75
Protestation of 1641, 55

Renshaw, James, 66, 67
Richardson, Edward (?), 59
Riding the Stang, 80
Roads, Back Lane (Hawthorn Lane),
  18
  Edge Lane, 18, 90
  Roman, 2, 19
  Trafford Lane, 18
  Wilbraham Road, 91
Robin Hood Inn, 106
Royal Oak Inn, 106
Rush bearing, 78

St. Ambrose, Church & Parish, 46
St. Augustine's Church & Parish, 103
St. Barnabas Church, 104
St. Clement's, Parish, 68
  Old Church, 50, 64, 100
    closing, 101, 104
  New Church, 100
St. John's, Church & Parish, 103
St. Werburgh's, Church & Parish, 70,
  104
Sale ees, 3
Salford Hundred, 5, 7
Salter, Rev. John, 63
Scaffold Field, 75, 83
Scholes, Rev. Jeremy, 59
Seale, 15
Souling, 82

Southern Cemetery, 112
Sparrow Heads, 78
Stocks, 80
Stretford Chapel, 18, 52
Stuart cause, 47, 63

Tansy pudding, 81
Tatton, William, 110
Taylor, Nathaniel, 55, 57
  Samuel, 58
Thomas, Rev. John, 60
Tithe Award map, 1845, 49, 82
Trafford family, 9, 11
Tramways, 92
Traveller's Rest (—Call) Inn, 106
Trevor Arms Hotel, 106
Tummusing, 82

Ughtred & Margaret, 14
  Sybil, daughter of, 15
Unitarian Chapel, 104
Usherwood, Margaret, Charity, 61

Vaughan, Father Jerome, 103

Waifs, 10
Wardley Hall, 46
Warre, Thomas de la, 17
Whitelock, Rev. R. H., 67
White Moss, 18
Wilton, Miss, 51
  Samuel, 51, 69
Withington, Matthew de, 7
  Roger de, 7
  Wilfrid (Wulfrith) de, 10
  William de, 7
Withington, Court Leet, 72
  etymology, 3
  Local Board, 94
    Chorlton Sewage Works, 98
  Manor of, 3
  Sanitary Authority, 94
    Preferential rating, 98
  Urban District of, 98
  Workhouse, 73
Worthington, Roger, 54
Wrestling, 75
Wright, Rev. Thomas, 60